THE
Garlic
COOKBOOK

LORNA RHODES

SMITHMARK

This edition published in 1994 by
SMITHMARK Publishers Inc.,
16 East 32nd Street,
New York, NY 10016.

3 5 7 9 8 6 4 2

SMITHMARK books are available for bulk purchase for sales promotion
and premium use. For details write or call the manager of special sales,
SMITHMARK Publishers Inc.,
16 East 32nd Street,
New York, NY 10016;
(212) 532-6600.

ISBN 0 8317 3885 5

CREDITS
COMMISSIONING EDITOR: *Will Steeds*
EDITOR: *Miranda Spicer*
DESIGN: *The Design Revolution, Brighton*
PHOTOGRAPHER: *Simon Butcher*
HOME ECONOMIST: *Lorna Rhodes*
STYLIST: *Hilary Guy*
COLOR SEPARATION: *P & W Graphics*

The publishers wish to thank Colin Boswell, Mersley Farms, Newchurch, Sandown, Isle of Wight
for his help and use of the photograph on page 10; and David Roser of The Garlic Research Bureau.

Printed in Singapore

Library of Congress Cataloging-in-Publication Data

Rhodes, Lorna.
    The garlic cookbook / Lorna Rhodes.
        p. cm.
    Includes index.
    ISBN 0-8317-3885-5 $9.98
    1. Cookery (Garlic) 2. Cookery, International. 3. Garlic.
    I. Title.
    TX819.G3R46 1994   94-26735
    641.6'526--dc20   CIP

ABOUT THE INGREDIENTS
As seasoning is a matter of personal taste, salt and pepper are not necessarily listed in the ingredients.
Try to obtain the best quality fresh produce.

CONTENTS

AUTHOR'S INTRODUCTION

I cannot imagine cooking without garlic because it transforms the taste of the simplest food to something really delicious. No other plant can perform this miracle of making bread, vegetables or meat so tasty. The cuisines in every part of the world make use of garlic in varying quantities, either subtly, so it hardly seems to be there, or in copious quantities, which surprisingly do not overpower the flavor of the food. Garlic can be used very successfully in large quantities. When it is prepared, either by slow cooking in oil or by boiling in water, the cloves are transformed into soft, sweet nuggets.

Garlic is inspirational. It conjures up a vision of appetizing food full of flavor, enjoyed in the company of friends and family, with wine and conversation flowing. It is reminiscent of eating together around the table at a leisurely pace, with time to savor the food – one of life's greatest pleasures.

When I studied home economics in the late 1960s, I was armed with my favorite (and for me the best) cookbook ever, *French Provincial Cooking* by Elizabeth David. What an influence this book had on me and my developing cooking talents! And it was also my introduction to cooking with garlic. Suddenly I found myself cooking garlic-laden, Mediterranean-style food as my parents had never known, much to the pleasure of my friends. My love of garlic has never faltered. While experimenting with Middle Eastern, Indian, Chinese and Thai cooking over the years, I have continued to be drawn to the rich and gutsy flavors of the Mediterranean. It is this love of garlic-enriched foods which brought me to write this book. But what a difficult task to choose recipes – there are so many!

Adding garlic to the simplest ingredients elevates them from the ordinary and prevents food from becoming boring and tasteless.

If you are lucky enough to obtain green garlic, which resembles leeks with fat bulbs, it's certainly worth using for its subtle flavor. Garlic is available throughout the year from different countries. Its appearance varies, from the size of the bulb, to the color of the skin. You may prefer to buy the attractive braids, especially if you use garlic frequently. Smoked garlic, with its golden skin, is more unusual and has a gentle garlic flavor.

For years the French and Italians have trusted garlic to give their cooking the distinctive flavor that is appreciated and copied all over the world. Both the Americans and British can still be inhibited about using the pungent bulb, but with an increasing love of foreign foods have come to appreciate its value. Mediterranean food has become a major influence on many diets with, for example, quick-cooking pasta dishes becoming family favorites. The whole ethos of the Mediterranean diet is now being recognized as beneficial to health, so it is no wonder that garlic is becoming an everyday ingredient in households across the globe.

Lorna Rhodes

INTRODUCTION

Since ancient times, people around the world have had a long and passionate relationship with garlic. As long ago as 5000 BC clay models of garlic bulbs were buried with Egyptians in their tombs, and more than 3000 years later Tutankhamun was buried with the real thing.

The countries of both the Greek and Roman empires made wide use of garlic, and the Old Testament tells us that the Israelites in the wilderness remembered: . . . "the fish, which we did eat freely; the cucumbers, and the melons, and the leeks, and the onions, and the garlick." (Numbers 11:5). The English name comes from the Anglo-Saxon "gar-leac" or spear plant, referring to the spear-shaped leaves.

The smell of garlic has been commented on profusely. Our modern-day enjoyment of this pungent bulb should not be denied, through fear of comparison with 16th-century Henry VI of France who chewed garlic and had "a breath that would fell an ox at twenty paces." Nevertheless, the smell of garlic has meant that the whims of polite society, whether Roman or Victorian,

ABOVE: *Garlic is widely used in the cuisines of countries bordering the Mediterranean.*

deemed garlic occasionally unfashionable. Mrs. Beeton wrote:

"The smell of this plant is generally considered offensive. It was in greater repute with our ancestors than it is with ourselves, although it is still used today as a seasoning or herb." This feeling was shared across the Atlantic in the USA, where it was considered, alongside olive oil, to be the most unpopular taste.

Garlic has been valued throughout history as a medicine as well as a food. It has held a reputation at one time or another as a remedy for virtually every illness – it has even been recommended as an aphrodisiac and a discourager of vampires. There can be little doubt that its more mainstream medicinal uses, both historically and in the present day, have proved both effective and beneficial.

Garlic's popularity is enjoying a revival. Nowadays, garlic festivals are held wherever it is grown commercially, usually in spring and early summer when the new season's crop comes in. In the USA, there is the Gilroy Festival, which attracts some 100,000 visitors. The Californian farming town calls itself "the world's garlic capital". In England, the Isle of Wight festival is at Newchurch in August, where the air is heavy with the aroma of garlic. Both Newchurch and Gilroy festivals have atmospheres like a mixture of a country fair, a gourmet food festival and a late 1960s pop festival. There is plenty of opportunity for visitors to participate in garlic tastings.

Countries where garlic is grown as an agricultural crop use it in abundance and appreciate its potency. Travel to the Mediterranean has re-emphasised garlic's influence, and has led to a resurgence in interest in garlicky food in the home countries of returning vacationers. The European, Central American and South American immigrants to the USA have brought garlic with them to expand and enliven local cooking. Throughout history, garlic has crossed centuries and borders, allowing us to enjoy its special flavor and qualities.

GARLIC AND HEALTH

Herbalists have used garlic since 1500 BC. From China, Greece, Egypt and the ancient kingdoms of Babylon, Sumeria and Mesopotamia, come complex recipes for all manner of diseases and health problems. All of these writings extol garlic as the king of medicinal plants, as well as making much of its virtues as a key ingredient in daily diet. But do these age-old stories of garlic's medicinal magic hold up under the rigorous scrutiny of science and medicine today?

Until very recently, scientists and researchers were sceptical about the diseases that garlic was claimed to treat. The list includes heart and arterial diseases; cholesterol control; reduction in internal blood clotting; prevention and cure of bacterial infections from Salmonella and Listeria organisms; antifungal activities against Candida species and so on. But is garlic really a cure-all?

Current rigorous scientific analysis and clinical research in hospitals and universities is clearly indicating that it does have a major and beneficial effect, both in remedying and preventing such key health problems. Garlic's secret is that inside each clove, contained in each of the individual cells, are two very important materials which are quite separate from one another in the growing plant. But the moment the clove is crushed or sliced these materials are brought together and a master material called allicin is created. The smell of fresh-cut garlic is the sign that allicin has been made. Allicin quickly breaks down when exposed to the air and through the heat of cooking, into over 70 different sulfur-bearing compounds. Many of these have specific effects on the body and this is why garlic is able to help with so many separate health problems.

In the late 1970s, a massive survey of the diets of 17 countries was carried out to establish which foods might explain the enormous differences between the incidences of cardiovascular diseases in Western countries in comparison with the low incidences in Mediterranean countries. The conclusion was that eating raw or cooked garlic and onions (in daily diet) was responsible – with the possible additional benefits of drinking a glass or two of red wine. The day-to-day consumption of garlic is now known to have major protective effects.

It is thought garlic can protect the arteries against fatty blockages; lower cholesterol levels if they are too high; help to prevent internal clots; kill stomach bugs; help with the symptoms of colds and 'flu,' and even stop mosquitoes from biting, because of the unpalatable sulfur molecules that develop on the skin when garlic is eaten regularly!

Garlic adds zest and flavor to food, and research indicates that if it is consumed regularly it may lead to improved general health.

THE CULTIVATION OF GARLIC

Garlic, *Allium sativum,* is part of the lily family that also includes onion, shallots, leeks, and chives. Garlic does not develop its full flavor until the bulbs have been allowed to dry and the outer layers appear papery and flaky. Single garlic cloves are planted annually in November. These are referred to as seed, by growers. Each bulb is made up of eight to ten cloves; the bulbs are divided into individual cloves which are planted. In the spring the plants produce long, pointed leaves known as garlic shoots. They can sometimes be found in specialist gourmet stores, but if you grow your own, all the better. Use them in salads or add them to egg dishes and sauces for a mild, fresh garlic flavor. Slightly older, firmer shoots can be used in Chinese cooking.

Green garlic is available at the start of the season, and again it can be found with specialist suppliers. If you have grown your own, lift it a month before harvesting. "Green" or "wet" garlic is the fresh white heads with green stems and juicy cloves, which have a mild flavor; its overall appearance is more like a leek. Its prized flavor is used in place of leeks or onions in soups, or cooked in soufflés. Green garlic will not keep for more than two or three weeks, whereas the dried heads keep for months.

At the beginning of July, the bulbs have finished swelling and the stems begin to dry out. When the bulbs are harvested the stems are left on and they are laid out in rows in the fields to dry in the sun. During this drying or curing time the cloves remain plump and juicy and the outer skin becomes flaky. The roots are then trimmed and the stems are snipped or braided. Between July and December the garlic comes from the northern hemisphere, from February onward the new crop comes from the southern hemisphere. There are differences in the shape, size and flavor, depending on where it is grown, and the color, which is either white, red, purple or pink.

Garlic needs plenty of sunshine, and grows well in warm countries. French garlic from the Mediterranean areas of southwest France and Provence has big juicy cloves and an excellent flavor, but does not keep well. Look out for the famous **Rose de Lautrec**, which is pink garlic from Lautrec. The garlic most commonly available during winter months is **Spanish Morado**, which has large cloves and keeps well. **Venetian Italian** garlic from the Po valley is a white dense bulb that also keeps well.

Chinese garlic has a symmetrical bulb in a thin purply or silver skin and has little flavor. Elephant garlic, which has a diameter of 3 to 4 inches, is not a true garlic, it originates from Southeast Asia and lacks the familiar strong flavor.

Oak-smoked garlic is now available in some gourmet stores. The garlic is smoked in a conventional

ABOVE: Newly harvested Isle of Wight garlic, in England.

smokehouse in a cold smoking process which takes up to 48 hours. The smoked bulbs are milder, give a hint of smoke and are supposed not to have an aftertaste.

GROW YOUR OWN GARLIC

Start with a healthy looking bulb with fat cloves. Separate the cloves and plant them individually, pointed end up, about 4 inches apart and 2 inches deep, in fall or early spring. They should be ready to harvest in July or August.

Select the best bulbs and replant them in the fall for bigger bulbs the next summer. To dry, clean off the soil from the bulbs and trim the roots. Put them in a sunny place where the air can circulate and leave for two to three weeks until the stems are very dry. If it rains, bring them inside. Trim the stems and either bunch together or braid together. Store in a cool, dry dark place.

COOKING WITH GARLIC

The famous cook Marcel Boulestin said:

"It is not an exaggeration to find that happiness and health is found where a lot of garlic is used in the kitchen."

In countries where garlic is grown, the local recipes include an abundance of garlic. Whole heads of garlic, roasted until they are soft and sweet, is a common sight. How much garlic is put in a dish is entirely a matter of taste, but the recipes in this book celebrate the use of lots of garlic.

The simplest way to peel a clove of garlic is to crush it beneath the blade of a heavy knife. There are some who swear by their garlic press and others who claim that it makes the fresh garlic taste bitter. The garlic press will produce a stronger garlic flavor. Many chefs prefer to mince rather than crush it. To hand-crush, remove the skin, take a little salt and either chop the garlic or mash with the flat blade of the knife, or mash in a pestle with a mortar. The salt will absorb the juices and make it easier to scoop the tiny garlic pieces off the board (it is advisable to keep a tiny wooden board solely for this purpose). Remember to use the salt as part of the seasoning to the dish. Alternatively, peel the skin off with a sharp knife, then cut the cloves into slices or slivers, or look out for a useful gadget which slices the cloves easily.

Whole cloves of garlic added to a dish impart less flavor than crushed or chopped ones. When boiling vegetables, add whole peeled cloves to the water to impart a subtle aroma. When roasting foods, add whole cloves, peeled or unpeeled; they can be served and mashed on the plate to be eaten with the meat or vegetables. For dishes that require a less-pronounced garlic flavor, poach the cloves for a few minutes in water to remove the strong pungency. Take this a step further and poach the cloves until they are tender, then press them through a sieve to make a mild, creamy purée. This purée appears in recipes in this book, but also try adding it to soups, sauces and dips.

There are many ways in which the flavor of garlic can be introduced to a dish without incorporating it into the food. Dressings can be infused with the flavor of garlic by adding crushed or chopped garlic to the mixture, then straining before use. Alternatively, rub the cut side of a clove of garlic around the salad bowl before adding the ingredients. For hot dishes, heat some garlic in the oil or butter to flavor it, but remove the garlic before adding other ingredients. Take care not to burn it – it will cook in seconds in hot oil or butter. In some recipes it is cooked very gently, in others it is allowed to turn golden, but never too brown, or it will taste bitter.

Roasted whole heads of garlic can be cooked around a joint of meat; allow one head per person. The inside becomes soft and tastes sweet and nutty, and can be squeezed from the skins and eaten with the meat and vegetables. Roast whole heads of garlic and use the purée in sauces or spread on toast. Special earthenware garlic roasters are available to cook one or more heads at a time. Alternatively, wrap the heads loosely in foil, drizzle with oil and bake in a medium-hot oven until soft. Slicing the top off the bulb before cooking makes it easier to squeeze out the purée once cooked. Garlic wrapped in foil can also be roasted on a barbecue.

HINTS AND TIPS

• Add peeled whole cloves of garlic to a jar of oil, refrigerate and keep for 2 to 3 days before using. Brush on foods before they are grilled, broiled or sautéed.
• Add peeled whole cloves of garlic to white-wine vinegar, and keep for 2 to 3 days before using in salad dressings.
• Bury 3 peeled and pressed cloves in half a cup of sea salt. Leave for a few days in a screw-topped jar. Remove garlic and use the salt as a seasoning.
• Make garlic purée by putting peeled cloves in a blender or food processor, add some olive oil and work until smooth. Store in a screw-topped jar for up to 5 days in the refrigerator. For a milder flavor, drain boiled garlic, then either mash it with a fork or push it through a strainer. It can be stored in a glass jar under a layer of olive oil, and will keep for 5 days in the refrigerator. Spread it on toast, add it to soups and sauces, stir it in to gravies, add it to vegetable purées or mashed potatoes.
• Peel 4 heads of garlic. Place in a glass jar with 4-6 small red chilies. Heat $1^{1}/4$ cups cider vinegar with 1 tablespoon sugar and 2 teaspoons salt. Cool, then pour over the garlic, seal and leave for 1 week. Use in Thai or Mexican recipes.
• Peel 8 ounces garlic cloves, put in a pan and add enough oil to cover. Cook over medium heat for 20 minutes until tender. Cool, then pack in a jar. Keep it in the refrigerator and use within 5 days. Use on pizzas and add to pasta.
• Store a string of garlic in a cool dry place, not in a warm, steamy kitchen. Pull a head off as required and break open to release the cloves. Strings or braids of garlic are a good buy if you use lots of garlic; otherwise buy smaller quantities and store in an earthenware garlic cellar, which allows the air to circulate and protects the garlic from the light.
• If the garlic has sprouted, slice each clove in half, remove and discard the green shoot (the flavor of sprouted garlic can be bitter).

RIGHT: Left to right: (back row) garlic and thyme olive oil; garlic in white-wine vinegar; earthenware garlic cellars; (front row) garlic roaster; garlic purée; roasted garlic in oil; minced garlic; garlic and chilies in cider vinegar.

APPETIZERS

Begin a meal with a garlic-flavored dish guaranteed to whet the appetite. For an informal appetizer with a rich taste of garlic, try Roasted Garlic and Avocado Dip. For a dinner party, smoked salmon rolls filled with a creamy mousse have just a subtle hint of garlic.

AïOLI WITH CRUDITÉS

6 cloves GARLIC, PEELED
2 EGG YOLKS
1 teaspoon DIJON MUSTARD
2/3 cup OLIVE OIL
2/3 cup PEANUT OIL
2 teaspoons LEMON JUICE

Crudités
PREPARED RAW VEGETABLES, SUCH AS
CARROT AND CELERY STICKS AND RADISHES

Ensure the ingredients for the aïoli are at room temperature, then put the garlic, egg yolks and mustard in a blender or food processor. With the motor running, add the oils a few drops at a time until the mixture starts to thicken. Increase the flow of oil until it is all incorporated, then beat in the lemon juice. Season with salt and pepper. Transfer to a bowl, cover and chill. Prepare a selection of colorful fresh crudités to serve with the aïoli.   SERVES 4-6

EGGPLANT ROLLS WITH GARLIC-TOMATO SAUCE

Sauce
2 tablespoons OLIVE OIL
3 cloves GARLIC, CRUSHED
3 cups SKINNED AND CHOPPED RIPE PLUM
TOMATOES
1/2 teaspoon DRIED BASIL
2 tablespoons DRY WHITE WINE

Eggplant Rolls
2 x 8-ounce EGGPLANTS
6 tablespoons OLIVE OIL
5 ounces SOFT MILD GOAT CHEESE
2 TOMATOES, SKINNED AND CHOPPED
a few fresh BASIL LEAVES, SHREDDED
flakes of PARMESAN CHEESE, TO GARNISH

To make the sauce, simmer all the ingredients together for 20 minutes. Strain, season and set aside.

Cut the eggplants lengthwise into eight 1/4-inch slices. Place in a large colander, sprinkle with salt and leave to drain for 30 minutes. Rinse and pat dry.

Preheat the oven to 375°F. Heat 2 tablespoons of the oil in a skillet. Add a layer of eggplant and fry on each side until just golden. Drain on paper towels. Repeat with more oil and slices. When cooked, spread the goat cheese on the eggplant slices, top with tomato and add some basil. Roll up. Place in a baking dish and bake for 15-20 minutes. Garnish and serve with a pool of warm tomato sauce.   SERVES 4

TOP: Aïoli with Crudités
BOTTOM: Eggplant Rolls with Garlic-Tomato Sauce

GARLICKY SALMON KEBABS

1¹/4 *pounds* SALMON FILLETS, SKINNED

16 RAW JUMBO SHRIMP OR TIGER PRAWNS, SHELLED

2 *tablespoons* SOY SAUCE

1 *tablespoon* LIME JUICE

3 *cloves* GARLIC, FINELY CHOPPED

1 *tablespoon* SUNFLOWER OIL

SHREDDED LETTUCE, TO SERVE

Soak 8 bamboo skewers in water before using. Cut the salmon into 1-inch cubes. Divide between the bamboo skewers and thread onto them with the shrimp. Preheat the broiler. In a small bowl, mix the soy sauce, lime juice, garlic and oil together; use to brush the kebabs. Broil for 5-6 minutes, turning and brushing with sauce. Serve on shredded lettuce.

SERVES 4

SMOKED SALMON ROLLS WITH GARLIC MOUSSE

Any left-over mousse can be served the next day with Melba toast.

³/4 *cup* CANNED BEEF CONSOMMÉ

1 *teaspoon* UNFLAVORED GELATIN

5 *ounces* SOFT CHEESE WITH GARLIC AND HERBS

4 *tablespoons* FROMAGE FRAIS

1 *clove* GARLIC, CRUSHED

8 *ounces* SMOKED SALMON, SLICED

LEMON TWISTS AND FRESH PARSLEY SPRIGS, TO GARNISH

To make the garlic mousse, heat the consommé. Sprinkle the gelatin onto 1 tablespoon of water and leave until spongy, then stir into the consommé to dissolve. Leave to cool. Pour into a blender or food processor. Add the cheese, fromage frais and garlic and blend until smooth. Pour into a bowl and chill until set.

Cut the slices of smoked salmon into eight 2¹/2 -inch-wide pieces. Place a tablespoonful of mousse at the end of each salmon piece and roll up. Serve 2 rolls per portion, garnished with lemon twists and parsley.

SERVES 4

SHRIMP IN GARLIC BUTTER

¹/2 *cup* BUTTER, SOFTENED

4 *cloves* GARLIC, CRUSHED WITH SALT

¹/2 *teaspoon* GRATED LEMON PEEL

1 *tablespoon* LEMON JUICE

3 *tablespoons* CHOPPED FRESH PARSLEY

FRESHLY GROUND BLACK PEPPER

12 *ounces* RAW JUMBO SHRIMP OR TIGER PRAWNS, SHELLED

Put the butter in a bowl. Add the garlic, lemon peel and juice and parsley; season with pepper. Beat well. Form into a roll on cling film. Wrap it up and refrigerate.

Divide the shrimp between 4 individual baking dishes. Slice the garlic butter and cover the shrimp with it. Place under a hot broiler and broil for 10 minutes, turning after 5 minutes. Serve with bread to mop up the juices.

SERVES 4

TOP: Garlicky Salmon Kebabs, Smoked Salmon Rolls with Garlic Mousse
BOTTOM: Shrimp in Garlic Butter

PORK AND GARLIC PÂTÉ

This pâté can be made in advance and kept for up to 4 days in the refrigerator.

1/4 cup BUTTER OR MARGARINE

1 MEDIUM ONION, CHOPPED

1/2 cup CHOPPED CELERY

1 1/2 cups CHOPPED MUSHROOMS

4 ounces RINDLESS SLAB BACON

4 fat cloves GARLIC, ROUGHLY CHOPPED

1/2 pound PIG'S, OR LAMB'S LIVER

1 EGG, BEATEN

2 tablespoons FRESH CHOPPED THYME OR
1 teaspoon DRIED THYME

2 tablespoons CHOPPED FRESH PARSLEY

1 pound GROUND PORK

2 tablespoons BRANDY

2 BAY LEAVES

Melt the butter in a large skillet. Add the onion, celery, mushrooms, bacon and garlic and cook for 8-10 minutes until softened. Leave to cool, then transfer to the bowl of a blender or food processor.

Preheat the oven to 325°F. Roughly chop the liver, add to the blender with the egg and purée. Transfer to a bowl. Add the herbs, pork and brandy. Season to taste. Stir until well blended. Spoon into a 5-cup baking dish or bread pan and top with 2 bay leaves. Cover with foil. Stand the dish in a roasting pan half-full of water and cook for 2 hours. Cool. Place a weight on top of the pâté and refrigerate overnight.

Cut into slices and serve with toast or crusty bread.

SERVES 8

BRIE AND GARLIC FONDUE

6 cloves GARLIC, PEELED

1/2 cup DRY WHITE WINE

2/3 cup LIGHT CREAM

12 ounces BRIE, RIND REMOVED

1 tablespoon CORNSTARCH

2 tablespoons BRANDY

CUBES OF FRENCH BREAD, TO SERVE

Put the garlic in a small pan, cover with water and simmer for 10 minutes until tender. Press the cloves through a strainer.

Pour the wine and cream into the fondue pot. Add the garlic purée and heat until bubbling. Cut the cheese into small pieces, add to the pot and stir until melted.

In a small bowl, blend the cornstarch and brandy together. Add to the pan and continue to cook for 2 minutes, stirring constantly until thick and creamy. Serve with cubes of French bread.

SERVES 4

RIGHT: Pork and Garlic Pâté

ROASTED GARLIC AND AVOCADO DIP

1 large head GARLIC
1 tablespoon OLIVE OIL
4 ounces MEDIUM-FAT CREAM CHEESE
2/3 cup SOUR CREAM
1 RIPE AVOCADO
1 tablespoon LEMON JUICE
2 tablespoons FINELY CHOPPED SCALLION
(OPTIONAL)

Preheat the oven to 400°F. Remove the papery outer skin from the head of garlic, without separating the cloves. Cut off 1/4 inch from the stem end. Place on foil, drizzle the oil over and loosely wrap up. Alternatively, use a garlic roaster. Bake for 40 minutes, until the cloves are soft. Cool.

Squeeze the garlic to remove the cloves from the skin. Put in a blender or food processor with the cream cheese and sour cream. Purée until smooth. Scoop out the flesh from the avocado. Add to the cream and cheese mixture with the lemon juice and process again until just smooth. Season. Stir in the onion, if using.   SERVES 6

MUSHROOMS TRIFOLATI

The Italian way of cooking vegetables in olive oil, garlic and parsley is described as "trifolati", where the name of this dish comes from.

6 tablespoons OLIVE OIL
4 cloves GARLIC, FINELY CHOPPED
4 cups SLICED BROWN MUSHROOMS
4 cups SLICED BUTTON MUSHROOMS
3 tablespoons CHOPPED FRESH PARSLEY

Heat the oil in a large skillet over medium heat. Add the garlic and cook for a few seconds to release the aroma. Increase the heat, add the mushrooms and quickly stir so they evenly absorb the oil. Toss the mushrooms in the pan for 4-5 minutes until tender. Season. Stir in the parsley, then spoon into a serving dish. Cool. Serve at room temperature.   SERVES 6

BRUSCHETTA WITH TOMATOES

This Italian garlic bread uses olive oil instead of butter, and the addition of tomatoes makes it a substantial appetizer.

3 LARGE, VERY RIPE TOMATOES, SKINNED
CIABATTA BREAD OR FRENCH BREAD
3 large cloves GARLIC, PEELED
1/2 teaspoon SALT
4 tablespoons EXTRA-VIRGIN OLIVE OIL
1 SMALL RED ONION, CHOPPED
SMALL BASIL LEAVES, TO GARNISH

Roughly chop the tomatoes. Cut the bread into diagonal slices, 1/2 inch thick. Mash the garlic with the salt to form a paste. Put in a bowl and mix with the olive oil. Broil the bread on both sides. Brush one side of each slice of bread with garlic mixture. Top with tomato, onion and basil leaves. Serve immediately.   SERVES 4

TOP: Roasted Garlic and Avocado Dip
BOTTOM: Mushrooms Trifolati

SOUPS

Generous amounts of garlic are added to these soups, which range from a Provençal pistou to Chinese Noodle Soup. Garlic Soup calls for smoked garlic which can be used to vary the flavor of all soups, but if this is not available use a head of dried or fresh garlic instead.

PISTOU

This hearty soup originates from Provence. It is given extra flavor by the addition of pistou sauce made with garlic, basil, olive oil and Parmesan cheese, which also gives the soup its name.

2 tablespoons OLIVE OIL

1 SMALL ONION, CHOPPED

3 cloves GARLIC, FINELY CHOPPED

2 SMALL LEEKS, THINLY SLICED

2 stalks CELERY, CHOPPED

5 cups CHICKEN OR VEGETABLE STOCK

6 ounces FRENCH-STYLE GREEN BEANS, CUT INTO SHORT PIECES

2 SMALL ZUCCHINI, DICED

1 SMALL POTATO, DICED

1 x 8-ounce CAN CRUSHED TOMATOES

1 x 15 1/2 -ounce CAN NAVY BEANS, DRAINED

1/3 cup SMALL PASTA SHAPES

SALT AND PEPPER

Pistou Sauce

4 cloves GARLIC

LARGE BUNCH BASIL LEAVES

3 tablespoons PINE NUTS

3 tablespoons EXTRA-VIRGIN OLIVE OIL

3 tablespoons FRESHLY GRATED PARMESAN CHEESE

To make the soup, heat the oil in a large saucepan. Add the onion and cook until softened. Add the garlic, leeks and celery and cook for 2 minutes, stirring occasionally. Pour in the stock, add the rest of the vegetables and simmer for 15 minutes. Stir in the pasta and continue to cook for 10-15 minutes until the pasta is *al dente*. Season to taste.

While the soup is simmering, make the pistou sauce. Pound the garlic in a mortar until crushed, then add the basil and pine nuts and pound to a paste. Alternatively, purée in a small blender or food processor. Mix in the oil, a little at a time. Finally, stir in the Parmesan. Serve with the pistou sauce swirled on top of bowls of hot soup.　　　　SERVES 6

RIGHT: Pistou

GARLIC SOUP

To garnish the soup, cut small shapes from 2 slices of white bread and fry in the residual garlic oil until golden. Dry on paper towels.

1 head OAK-SMOKED GARLIC
2 tablespoons OLIVE OIL
3 tablespoons BUTTER
1 LARGE ONION, FINELY CHOPPED
3 cups CHICKEN STOCK
4 slices DAY-OLD CRUSTLESS WHITE BREAD
2/3 cup LIGHT CREAM
1 ounce BLANCHED ALMONDS, FINELY CHOPPED
CHOPPED FRESH PARSLEY OR CHIVES, TO GARNISH

Separate the garlic cloves, removing the papery skins. Heat the oil in a pan, add the garlic and cook for 10-15 minutes until tender. Remove from the heat. Cool, then skin. Roughly chop the flesh. Melt the butter in a large saucepan, add the garlic and onion, cover and cook over low heat for 10-15 minutes until the onion is soft. Pour in the stock, add the bread and simmer for 30 minutes. Transfer the soup to a blender or food processor. Add the cream and almonds and blend until smooth. Garnish and serve. SERVES 4

CHINESE NOODLE SOUP

5 cups CHICKEN STOCK
1-inch piece FRESH GINGERROOT, FINELY CHOPPED
4 cloves GARLIC, FINELY CHOPPED
1 cup SLICED BUTTON MUSHROOMS
1 tablespoon ASIAN FISH SAUCE
2 ounces RICE VERMICELLI NOODLES
3 SCALLIONS, THINLY SLICED
1 tablespoon SHREDDED FRESH CILANTRO LEAVES, TO GARNISH

Put the stock, ginger and garlic in a saucepan. Slowly bring to a boil. Add the mushrooms to the pan with fish sauce, cover and simmer for 10 minutes.

Meanwhile, soak the noodles for 10 minutes. Drain the noodles, add to the soup and simmer for 3 minutes until warm and soft. Scatter the scallions over the soup and garnish. SERVES 4

BEET AND GARLIC SOUP

2 tablespoons BUTTER
1 ONION, CHOPPED
4 ounces GARLIC
1 pound RAW BEETS, PEELED AND CUT INTO SMALL DICE
1 LARGE POTATO, PEELED AND DICED
3 3/4 cups VEGETABLE STOCK
CHOPPED FRESH PARSLEY, TO GARNISH
SOUR CREAM, TO SERVE

Melt the butter in a large pan. Add the onion and cook for 5 minutes to soften. Add the garlic, beets and potato, cover the pan and sweat for 3 minutes. Pour in the stock and simmer the soup for 1 1/2 hours until the beets are tender. Blend until smooth, then strain. Season if needed. Garnish with parsley and serve with swirls of sour cream. SERVES 6

TOP: Garlic Soup
BOTTOM: Beet and Garlic Soup

BOUILLABAISSE

Authentic bouillabaisse uses red gunard, conger eel and rascasse, but a carefully chosen selection of fresh white fish and shellfish is an acceptable alternative. It is accompanied by a spicy, hot condiment called rouille.

2 pounds MIXED WHITE FISH, DRAWN

1 pound MIXED SHELLFISH

4 tablespoons OLIVE OIL

1 LARGE ONION, CHOPPED

white parts of 2 SMALL LEEKS, CHOPPED

4 heads GARLIC, HALVED HORIZONTALLY

1 SMALL BULB FENNEL, SLICED

5 RIPE TOMATOES, SKINNED AND CHOPPED

3 STRIPS ORANGE PEEL

good pinch SAFFRON THREADS

6 1/4 cups HOT FISH STOCK (MADE FROM FISH TRIMMINGS)

1 sprig FRESH THYME

1 BAY LEAF

CHOPPED FRESH PARSLEY, TO GARNISH

slices FRENCH BREAD, TOASTED, TO SERVE

Rouille

3 SLICES WHITE BREAD, CRUSTS REMOVED, AND SOAKED IN MILK

4 cloves GARLIC

1 teaspoon PAPRIKA

1/2 teaspoon CAYENNE PEPPER

5 tablespoons OLIVE OIL

To make the *rouille,* squeeze the milk from the bread. Put the bread in a small blender or food processor with the garlic and spices and work to a thick paste. Gradually add the oil until it has the consistency of thick cream. Set aside.

Clean and prepare the fish; remove the skin, fins and bones and cut into chunks. The shellfish can be left in their shells (remove heads if preferred). Discard any mussels or clams that do not close when tapped.

Heat the oil in a very large pan. Add the onion, leeks, garlic and fennel and cook until golden. Add the tomatoes, orange peel, saffron, fish stock and herbs. Bring to a boil and boil until the oil mixes into the stock and does not float. Reduce the heat, add the firm white fish and simmer for 8 minutes. Add the shellfish and delicate white fish and cook for 5 minutes longer. Season if needed. Remove the orange peel and bay leaf. Discard any mussels or clams which have failed to open. Garnish with parsley.

Spread the *rouille* on toast and place in the bottom of deep bowls, then pour in the bouillabaisse, or serve the toast separately to float on top.   SERVES 6

RIGHT: Bouillabaisse

RED PEPPER AND TOMATO SOUP

1 pound RED BELL PEPPERS
2 tablespoons OLIVE OIL
1 RED ONION, CHOPPED
3 cloves GARLIC, CRUSHED
3 cups SKINNED AND CHOPPED RIPE TOMATOES
2 1/2 cups VEGETABLE STOCK
1/2 teaspoon DRIED BASIL
CHOPPED FRESH PARSLEY OR BASIL, TO GARNISH

Broil the peppers under a hot broiler, turning them until they are charred on all sides. Place in a plastic bag and set aside for 20 minutes. Heat the oil in a large saucepan, add the onion and garlic and cook gently to soften. Stir in the tomatoes, stock and basil. Simmer for 15 minutes.

Remove the peppers from the bag, peel and discard the skins and seeds. Chop the flesh and add to the pan. Continue to simmer the soup for 15 minutes. Purée until smooth in a blender or food processor. If the soup is too thick, add a little water. Reheat the soup and season to taste. Garnish with chopped parsley or basil.

SERVES 4

TUSCAN BEAN AND GARLIC SOUP

1 1/3 cups DRIED CANNELLINI OR OTHER WHITE BEANS, SOAKED OVERNIGHT OR
2 x 15 1/2-ounce CANS CANNELLINI BEANS, DRAINED
3 tablespoons OLIVE OIL
2 cups CHOPPED WHITE PARTS OF LEEKS
3 large cloves GARLIC, CHOPPED
3 3/4 cups CHICKEN STOCK
2 tablespoons CHOPPED FRESH PARSLEY

If using dried, soaked beans, drain and rinse them in cold water, then put them in a large saucepan. Add enough water to cover them by at least 3 inches. Bring to a boil, then simmer for about 1 1/2 hours until tender. Keep them in their liquid until required, then drain.

Heat the oil in a large pan, add the leeks and cook for 3-4 minutes longer to soften. Stir in the garlic, cook over low heat for 3-4 minutes longer but do not let the garlic color. Add the stock and half of the drained cooked or canned beans and simmer for 30 minutes. Purée in a blender or food processor. Return to the pan, add the rest of the beans, season and simmer for 20 minutes. Stir in the parsley. Serve with crusty bread, such as Italian ciabatta bread. SERVES 4-5

TOP: Red Pepper and Tomato Soup
BOTTOM: Tuscan Bean and Garlic Soup

SALADS

Salads can be a fresh and light accompaniment, or a main course in themselves. For just a hint of garlic, rub the inside of the salad bowl with a cut clove. To increase the flavor, use a garlic dressing and, for real garlic lovers, scatter raw garlic directly onto the salad.

PASTA SALAD WITH BASIL AND GARLIC DRESSING

2 cups PASTA SHAPES
2 LARGE RED BELL PEPPERS, ROASTED
(SEE PAGE 28)
1/3 cup PINE NUTS, LIGHTLY TOASTED

Dressing
1 ounce BASIL LEAVES, RINSED AND DRIED
4 cloves GARLIC
2 tablespoons WHITE-WINE VINEGAR
1 tablespoon DIJON MUSTARD
1/2 cup OLIVE OIL

Cook the pasta in a large pan of boiling salted water until *al dente*. Drain, rinse in cold water and drain well. Put in a large bowl. Peel the peppers, discard the seeds and cut into small dice. Add to the pasta with the pine nuts. Chop the basil and garlic using a small blender or food processor. Add the vinegar and mustard, then with the motor running, add the oil. Season with a little salt and pepper. Spoon over the salad and toss.   SERVES 6

GREEN SALAD WITH GARLIC DRESSING

2 heads CRISP LETTUCE, RINSED
1/2 head LOLLO BIANCO, RINSED
1 bunch WATERCRESS, TRIMMED AND RINSED
1/2 CUCUMBER, SLICED
1 GREEN BELL PEPPER, SEEDED AND SLICED
2 tablespoons CHOPPED FRESH HERBS, SUCH AS CHIVES
AND PARSLEY
EDIBLE FLOWERS, TO GARNISH

Dressing
6 tablespoons OLIVE OIL
2 tablespoons WINE VINEGAR
2 cloves GARLIC, CRUSHED
1/2 teaspoon DIJON MUSTARD
1/2 teaspoon SUGAR

Dry the salad leaves in a spinner, tear into small pieces and put in a large bowl with the watercress, cucumber, pepper and herbs. Put the ingredients for the dressing in a screw-topped jar, season with salt and pepper and shake well until mixed. Pour over the salad. Toss and serve immediately with crusty bread to mop up the garlic dressing. Garnish with edible flowers, such as borage if available.   SERVES 4-6

TOP: *Pasta Salad with Basil and Garlic Dressing*
BOTTOM: *Green Salad with Garlic Dressing*

RICE, EGGPLANT AND GARLIC SALAD

This salad does not need a dressing because the eggplant releases some of the oil that it has been cooked in to moisten the other ingredients.

1 LARGE EGGPLANT

5 tablespoons OLIVE OIL

15 cloves GARLIC, CHOPPED

1 cup LONG-GRAIN AND WILD RICE MIXED

4 TOMATOES, DICED

1 SMALL RED ONION, FINELY CHOPPED

2 tablespoons CHOPPED FRESH PARSLEY

Cut the eggplant into $1/2$-inch dice, sprinkle with salt and set aside for 30 minutes. Heat 2 tablespoons oil in a small pan. Add the garlic and cook gently for about 15 minutes until golden and tender. Cool.

Meanwhile, cook the rice mixture in boiling salted water until tender. Rinse under cold water, drain and put in a large bowl. Add the garlic to the rice with the tomatoes and onion.

Rinse the eggplant, then dry on paper towels. Heat 3 tablespoons of the oil with any oil from cooking the garlic in a large skillet. Add the eggplant and sauté until golden and tender. Cool. Stir into the rice mixture with the parsley. SERVES 4-6

CORN AND PEPPER SALAD WITH GARLIC SALSA

A colorful salad with a slightly spicy flavor which makes a good accompaniment to barbecued food.

12 ounces FROZEN WHOLE-KERNEL CORN

1 GREEN BELL PEPPER, SEEDED

1 RED BELL PEPPER, SEEDED

1/2 CUCUMBER, DICED

Salsa

4 or 5 cloves GARLIC, CHOPPED

2 tablespoons RED-WINE VINEGAR

1/2 teaspoon GROUND CUMIN

1/2 teaspoon DRIED OREGANO

SALT

1 GREEN CHILI, SEEDED AND CHOPPED

SALT

5 tablespoons OLIVE OIL

5 TOMATOES, SKINNED, SEEDED AND ROUGHLY CHOPPED

small bunch FRESH CILANTRO, CHOPPED

Put the corn in a pan. Cover with water and bring to a boil, then simmer for 2-3 minutes. Drain, then cool, and put in a bowl. Cut the peppers into small dice and add to the corn with the cucumber.

To make the salsa, put the garlic, vinegar, cumin, oregano, chili and a little salt into a small blender or food processor. Blend until finely chopped. Add the oil and blend to mix. Add the tomatoes but only blend in short bursts, so they still look partly chopped. Stir into the salad with the cilantro. SERVES 6-8

TOP: Rice, Eggplant and Garlic Salad
BOTTOM: Corn and Pepper Salad with Garlic Salsa

CALIFORNIAN CHICKEN AND AVOCADO SALAD

4 LARGE, BONELESS CHICKEN BREAST HALVES
1 tablespoon OLIVE OIL
1 teaspoon DRIED OREGANO
SALT AND PEPPER
2 LARGE AVOCADOS
3 TOMATOES, DICED
1 tablespoon CHOPPED FRESH MINT OR PARSLEY
SELECTION OF MIXED LETTUCES, SUCH AS LOLLO ROSSO, FRISÉE OR OAK LEAF
1 SMALL RED ONION, CUT INTO RINGS, TO GARNISH

Dressing
2 cloves GARLIC, PREFERABLY OAK SMOKED
4 tablespoons OLIVE OIL
1 tablespoon RED-WINE VINEGAR
juice and grated peel of 1 SMALL ORANGE

Rub the skinless side of the chicken with oil, oregano and salt and pepper. Heat a ridged griddle or broiler and cook the chicken for 15 minutes, turning until cooked through and the juices run clear when each piece is pierced with the tip of a knife. Set aside to cool.

Meanwhile, to make the dressing, crush the garlic and mix to a paste with a little olive oil. Beat in the red-wine vinegar, remaining oil, the grated orange peel and 3 tablespoons orange juice. Season.

Remove the chicken skin, cut into thin strips and mix with the dressing. Halve the avocados and discard the seeds. Use a small melon-ball cutter to scoop the flesh into balls. Mix into the chicken with the tomatoes and mint. Toss gently. Arrange the lettuce leaves on plates. Top with the salad and garnish with onion rings.

SERVES 4

POTATO SALAD WITH GARLIC MAYONNAISE

1¹/2 pounds SMALL NEW POTATOES OR OTHER VARIETY
4 tablespoons MAYONNAISE
3 tablespoons PLAIN YOGURT OR SOUR CREAM
1 tablespoon WHITE-WINE VINEGAR
2 cloves GARLIC, CRUSHED
SALT AND PEPPER
2 tablespoons SNIPPED FRESH CHIVES, TO GARNISH

Put the potatoes in a pan of cold water, bring to a boil and simmer for 15-20 minutes or until tender. Drain. Leave very small potatoes whole; large ones can be halved or quartered. Put potatoes in a large bowl.

In a small bowl, mix together the mayonnaise, yogurt, vinegar and garlic. Season. Fold into the potatoes while they are still warm. Garnish and serve.

For a more substantial salad, add 1 cup cooked diced smoked pork sausage, or 4 ounces sliced pepperoni, to the potatoes.

SERVES 4

RIGHT: Californian Chicken and Avocado Salad

SWEET PEPPER SALAD

2 LARGE RED BELL PEPPERS
2 LARGE YELLOW BELL PEPPERS
6 *tablespoons* VIRGIN OLIVE OIL
4 *cloves* GARLIC, CUT INTO SLIVERS

To Garnish
1 *tablespoon* CHOPPED FRESH FLAT-LEAVED PARSLEY
RIPE OLIVES

Preheat the broiler to high. Broil the peppers, turning them until the skins are black and blistered on all sides. Place in a plastic bag, seal and leave to cool for 20 minutes. Peel off the skins, discard stems and seeds. Cut the flesh into strips and arrange in a shallow dish. Drizzle the olive oil over. Scatter the garlic over and marinate for at least 2 hours at room temperature.

To store overnight or for up to 3 days, cover with plastic wrap and refrigerate. Bring to room temperature and garnish with parsley and olives to serve.   SERVES 4-6

SALAD NIÇOISE

This colorful salad makes a lunch dish or first course. Serve with French bread, sun-dried tomato bread or olive bread, if available.

4 *ounces* FRENCH-STYLE GREEN BEANS, COOKED
AND COOLED
8 *ounces* BABY NEW POTATOES, COOKED AND
COOLED
6 SCALLIONS, CHOPPED
6 1/2 CHERRY TOMATOES, HALVED, IF WISHED
1 x 6 1/8-*ounce* CAN TUNA, DRAINED AND FLAKED
1/2 *cup* RIPE OLIVES, STONED
1 HEAD CRISP LETTUCE, RINSED AND DRIED
3 HARD-BOILED EGGS, SHELLED
1 x 2-*ounce* CAN ANCHOVIES, DRAINED

Dressing
2 *cloves* GARLIC
2 ANCHOVY FILLETS
2 *teaspoons* BALSAMIC VINEGAR
1 *tablespoon* LEMON JUICE
1/2 *teaspoon* DIJON MUSTARD
6 *tablespoons* OLIVE OIL

To make the dressing, purée the garlic, the anchovies (taken from the can listed with the other ingredients), vinegar, lemon juice and mustard in a blender or food processor. With the motor still running, add the oil.

Cut the beans into short pieces and halve or quarter the potatoes. In a large bowl, combine all the salad ingredients, except the lettuce, eggs and anchovies. Add the dressing and toss. Arrange the lettuce on a platter and spoon the salad over. Quarter the eggs and arrange on the salad. Halve the anchovy fillets lengthwise and arrange in a crisscross pattern on top.   SERVES 4

TOP: *Sweet Pepper Salad*
BOTTOM: *Salad Niçoise*

SUMMER SALAD WITH GARLIC CROUTONS

1 large clove GARLIC, HALVED
2 handfuls FRISÉE LETTUCE LEAVES
1 head CRISP GREEN LETTUCE, RINSED AND DRIED
1 RED BELL PEPPER, SEEDED AND DICED
1/2 CUCUMBER, PEELED AND DICED
1 head FENNEL, SLICED
1/2 bunch SCALLIONS, TRIMMED AND CHOPPED
3 TOMATOES, CUT INTO STRIPS

Dressing
3 tablespoons SUNFLOWER OIL
1 tablespoon OLIVE OIL
1 tablespoon RED-WINE VINEGAR
1/2 teaspoon DIJON MUSTARD

Croutons
2 LARGE THICK SLICES BREAD
VEGETABLE OIL FOR FRYING
3 cloves GARLIC, VERY FINELY CHOPPED
1/2 teaspoon SALT

Rub the inside of the salad bowl with the halved clove of garlic. Prepare the salad ingredients and put in the bowl. Mix the dressing ingredients together in a screw-top jar.

To make the croutons, remove the crusts from the bread and cut into small cubes. Heat enough oil in a pan to deep-fry the croutons. Add the cubed bread and fry until golden and crisp. Remove with a slotted spoon and drain well on paper towels.

Mix the garlic and salt together, then put in a bowl, add the croutons and toss. Leave to cool. Add the dressing to the salad and toss together. Scatter the croutons over. For an extra garlicky salad, scatter the chopped garlic over the salad.   SERVES 4-6

BEAN AND GARLIC SALAD

Pinto or cranberry beans look attractive with the green beans but use other varieties if preferred.

1 1/3 cups DRIED PINTO OR CRANBERRY BEANS, SOAKED OVERNIGHT OR
2 x 15 1/2-ounce CANS PINTO BEANS, DRAINED
SALT
8 ounces GREEN BEANS

Dressing
4 tablespoons OLIVE OIL
4 or 5 cloves GARLIC, FINELY CHOPPED
1 tablespoon RED-WINE VINEGAR
2 tablespoons CHOPPED FRESH PARSLEY

Drain the soaked beans, cover with water and bring to a boil. Simmer until almost tender, about 1 hour. Add salt to taste and continue simmering until tender.

Meanwhile, trim the greeen beans and slice diagonally in thin strips. Cook in a little boiling salted water for 3-4 minutes. Drain both pans and put beans in a bowl.

To make the dressing, heat the oil in a small pan, add the garlic and cook until golden. Remove from the heat and, swirl in the vinegar. Pour over the beans and toss. Scatter the parsley over. Leave to cool and serve at room temperature.   SERVES 6-8

RIGHT: Summer Salad with Garlic Croutons

CHINESE CHICKEN SALAD

4 BONELESS, SKINLESS CHICKEN BREAST HALVES

1-inch piece FRESH GINGERROOT, CUT INTO STRIPS

2 cloves GARLIC, HALVED

Dressing

1 tablespoon SESAME OIL

2 tablespoons SUNFLOWER OIL

1 tablespoon SOY SAUCE

1 tablespoon RICE WINE, VINEGAR OR CIDER VINEGAR

2-3 cloves GARLIC, CRUSHED

1 teaspoon BOTTLED CHILI SAUCE

Salad

4 ounces BEAN SPROUTS, WASHED AND TRIMMED

1½ cups SLICED BUTTON MUSHROOMS

5 SCALLIONS, CHOPPED

4-inch piece CUCUMBER, SLICED OR DICED

1 GREEN BELL PEPPER, SEEDED AND CUT INTO THIN STRIPS

TOASTED OR BLACK SESAME SEEDS, TO GARNISH

Put the chicken in a pan and add just enough water to cover. Add the ginger and garlic and simmer for about 10 minutes until the juices run clear when each piece of chicken is pierced with the tip of a knife. Leave to cool in the liquid.

Cube the chicken and transfer to a large serving bowl. Mix the ingredients for the dressing together in a screw-top jar. Add the ingredients for the salad to the chicken and toss together with the dressing. Sprinkle with sesame seeds.

SERVES 4

WARM LENTIL SALAD

Puy lentils have a distinctive flavor, they are slate green in color and hold their shape during cooking. Serve warm with grilled or broiled meats.

1½ cups PUY LENTILS

2 BAY LEAVES

2 sprigs THYME

SALT

3 tablespoons OLIVE OIL

1 RED ONION, FINELY CHOPPED

1 LARGE CARROT, FINELY DICED

2 stalks CELERY, FINELY DICED

3 cloves GARLIC, THINLY SLICED

2 tablespoons BALSAMIC OR RED-WINE VINEGAR

3 tablespoons CHOPPED FRESH PARSLEY

Rinse the lentils, then put in a large saucepan with bay leaves and thyme and cover with cold water. Bring to a boil, then simmer for 15 minutes. Add salt to taste and simmer for 5-10 minutes longer until tender.

While the lentils are simmering, heat the oil in a large skillet. Add the onion, carrot and celery and cook gently for about 8 minutes until they begin to soften. Add the garlic and cook for 2 minutes longer. Drain the lentils, discard the herbs and stir the lentils into the vegetables with the vinegar and parsley.

SERVES 4

RIGHT: Chinese Chicken Salad

FISH DISHES

Many of these fish and seafood recipes have a strong Mediterranean flavor. They are inspired by the tastes and aromas of the cooking of warm, sun-drenched countries. All the ingredients are available from supermarkets or fish merchants.

SEAFOOD PAELLA

3 tablespoons OLIVE OIL

9 ounces MONKFISH FILLET, SKINNED, CUT INTO BITE-SIZE CHUNKS

1 ONION, CHOPPED

5 cloves GARLIC, THINLY SLICED

1 RED BELL PEPPER, SEEDED AND CHOPPED

1¼ cups RISOTTO RICE

3 cups FISH STOCK

²/₃ cup DRY WHITE WINE

few SAFFRON THREADS

14 ounces PREPARED MIXED SHELLFISH, SUCH AS COOKED MUSSELS, SQUID, SHRIMP AND SCALLOPS

4 ounces FROZEN PEAS

SALT AND PEPPER

To Garnish

sprigs FRESH PARSLEY

LEMON WEDGES

Heat the oil in a paella pan or large shallow flameproof casserole. Add the monkfish and fry over medium heat for 5 minutes. Remove with a slotted spoon and set aside. Add the onion, increase the heat and fry until soft. Stir in the garlic and pepper and stir-fry for 2 minutes. Add the rice and stir until it is coated with the onion mixture. Pour in the stock and wine, add the saffron and bring to a boil. Simmer, uncovered, for 20 minutes.

Add the monkfish and continue to simmer for 5-10 minutes longer until most of the stock has been absorbed and the rice is tender. Stir the prepared shellfish into the rice with the peas and cook for 5 minutes for the shellfish and peas to warm through. Add a little more stock if necessary. Season and garnish with parsley and lemon wedges. SERVES 4

RIGHT: Seafood Paella

MEDITERRANEAN FISH STEW

4 tablespoons OLIVE OIL
2¹/₂ cups PEELED AND DICED POTATOES
1 SMALL ONION, FINELY CHOPPED
1 RED BELL PEPPER, SEEDED AND SLICED
4 cloves GARLIC, THINLY SLICED
1 teaspoon PAPRIKA
3 cups SKINNED AND CHOPPED PLUM TOMATOES
1 cup DRY WHITE WINE
1 pound COD FILLET, SKINNED
6 ounces FROZEN RAW SHRIMP
CHOPPED PARSLEY, TO GARNISH

Heat the oil in a large saucepan or deep skillet. Add the potatoes, onion and red bell pepper and cook gently for 10 minutes, stirring constantly. Add the garlic and paprika and cook for 1 minute longer. Stir in the tomatoes, wine and ²/₃ cup water and simmer, uncovered, for about 25 minutes until the potatoes are just tender.

Cut the fish into large chunks, then add to the pan with the shrimp and simmer for 5-8 minutes until the fish begins to flake and the shrimp turn pink. Garnish with the parsley and serve. SERVES 4

SAUTÉED MONKFISH WITH NIÇOISE SAUCE

The very highly flavored sauce complements the firm texture of the fish. This recipe also works well with swordfish or tuna steaks.

¹/₃ cup RIPE OLIVES, PITTED
4 teaspoons SUN-DRIED TOMATO PASTE OR
3 or 4 SUN-DRIED TOMATOES IN OIL, DRAINED
2 teaspoons CAPERS, DRAINED
1 or 2 ANCHOVY FILLETS
4 tablespoons BUTTER
4 cloves GARLIC, CRUSHED
1 pound MONKFISH FILLETS, SKINNED AND CUT INTO ¹/₂-INCH SLICES
2 tablespoons CHOPPED FRESH PARSLEY, TO GARNISH

Put the olives, sun-dried tomato paste, capers and anchovies in a small blender or food processor and chop finely.

Melt the butter in a skillet. Add the garlic and cook gently for 1-2 minutes without letting the garlic brown. Add the fish and sauté for about 5-7 minutes until just beginning to flake.

Stir in the niçoise sauce and continue to cook for 3-4 minutes, turning the pieces of fish to coat with sauce. Garnish with parsley and serve immediately. SERVES 4

TOP: *Mediterranean Fish Stew*
BOTTOM: *Sautéed Monkfish with Niçoise Sauce*

MOULES MARINIÈRE

4 *pounds* MUSSELS
2 *or 3* SHALLOTS, FINELY CHOPPED
3 *cloves* GARLIC, FINELY CHOPPED
2 *tablespoons* CHOPPED FRESH PARSLEY
3/4 cup plus 2 tablespoons DRY WHITE WINE
2 *tablespoons* BUTTER
1 *tablespoon* ALL-PURPOSE FLOUR
PEPPER
EXTRA CHOPPED FRESH PARSLEY,
TO GARNISH

Scrape, scrub and thoroughly clean the mussels under running water. Pull away the beard and throw away any that are cracked, or that remain open when tapped. Put the shallots, garlic, parsley and wine into the largest pan possible and simmer for 10 minutes. Add the mussels, put the lid on and cook over a high heat for about 5 minutes. Shake the pan once or twice during cooking.

Mash the butter and flour together. Strain the cooking juices into another saucepan and boil for 3 minutes. Remove from the heat, then beat in the butter and flour paste, return to the heat and bring to a boil. Season, if needed, with pepper.

Lift the mussels into deep soup bowls, discarding any that have not opened. Pour the sauce over and sprinkle with parsley. Serve with crusty French bread.

SERVES 4 AS AN APPETIZER OR 2 AS A MAIN COURSE

SCALLOPS PROVENÇAL

Use queen scallops for this dish; they are small in size and have a wonderful flavor. Alternatively, use the larger size and cut them in half.

1¼ *pounds* QUEEN SCALLOPS
2 *tablespoons* OLIVE OIL
1 ONION, FINELY CHOPPED
4 *cloves* GARLIC, THINLY SLICED
3 *cups* SKINNED AND CHOPPED RIPE TOMATOES
1 *teaspoon* TOMATO PASTE
1 *teaspoon* FRESH THYME LEAVES
2/3 *cup* DRY WHITE WINE
SALT AND PEPPER
2 *tablespoons* CHOPPED FRESH PARSLEY, TO GARNISH

Rinse the scallops and leave the corals attached, then drain in a colander and trim off any black veins.

Heat the oil in a skillet and sauté the onion until softened. Add the garlic and after a few seconds stir in the tomatoes, tomato paste, thyme and wine. Simmer, uncovered, for 15-20 minutes until the sauce becomes pulpy. Season.

Stir in the scallops and cook for 3 minutes (any longer and they will become tough). Garnish and serve immediately.

SERVES 4

TOP: Scallops Provençal
Bottom: Moules Marinière

TROUT IN LEMON-GARLIC SAUCE

❧

Try this recipe with other small whole fish, such as small red snapper.

4 TROUT, DRESSED
2 tablespoons LEMON JUICE
coarsely grated peel of 1 LEMON
2 tablespoons BUTTER
20 cloves GARLIC, PEELED
1¼ cups LIGHT CREAM

Preheat the oven to 375°F. Slash the trout 2 or 3 times on each side, then place in a shallow baking dish in a single layer. Pour the lemon juice over, add the peel, dot with butter and tuck the cloves of garlic in between the fish. Cover with foil. Bake for about 25 minutes until the fish is tender and flakes easily.

Meanwhile, pour the cream into a small pan, and simmer until thick and reduced by about half; set aside. Pour off the juices from the fish. Remove the garlic. Press through a strainer and blend the purée back into the juices. Stir the mixture into the cream, reheat gently; do not boil. Serve the trout with the sauce. SERVES 4

FLOUNDER WITH LEEK AND GARLIC STUFFING

❧

6 *large* FLOUNDER FILLETS, SKINNED

Stuffing
8 ounces LEEKS, TRIMMED (LEAVE SOME OF THE
GREEN PARTS)
3½ *tablespoons* BUTTER
3 cloves GARLIC, FINELY CHOPPED OR
CRUSHED
2 tablespoons BLANCHED ALMONDS, FINELY GROUND
SALT AND PEPPER
¾ cup FRESH WHOLE-WHEAT BREAD CRUMBS
2 tablespoons SLIVERED ALMONDS
2 tablespoons CHOPPED FRESH PARSLEY

Preheat the oven to 375°F. Skin the fillets and divide each one along the central line into 2 smaller fillets. Quarter the leeks lengthwise, rinse and drain, then thinly slice.

Melt 2 tablespoons of the butter in a small pan, add the leeks and garlic, stir well and cook gently until the leeks are tender. Remove from the heat, stir in the ground almonds and season. Set aside to cool. Put a spoonful of the stuffing at the thick end of each flounder fillet, roll up and put in a buttered baking dish. Cover with foil and bake for 20 minutes.

Meanwhile, melt the remaining butter in a skillet. Add the crumbs and cook, stirring, until they start to crisp. Add the almonds and cook for 1-2 minutes until golden. Remove from the heat and add parsley. Remove the fish from the oven. Transfer to serving plates, spoon a little juice over and top with the golden crumbs. SERVES 4

TOP: Trout in Lemon-Garlic Sauce
BOTTOM: Flounder with Leek and Garlic Stuffing

HADDOCK WITH LIME AND CILANTRO

1 tablespoon SUNFLOWER OIL
8 SCALLIONS, FINELY CHOPPED
4 cloves GARLIC, FINELY CHOPPED
2 tablespoons CHOPPED FRESH CILANTRO
grated peel and juice of 2 LIMES
SALT AND PEPPER
4 THICK HADDOCK FILLETS, SKINNED

To Garnish
1 LIME, CUT INTO WEDGES
CILANTRO LEAVES

Preheat the oven to 375°F. Heat the oil in a small pan, add the scallions and garlic and cook for 1 minute. Remove from the heat and stir in the cilantro and lime peel and juice. Season.

Put the haddock fillets in a baking dish, spoon the topping over, cover and bake for 20 minutes until the fish is tender and the flesh flakes easily. Garnish with lime wedges and cilantro leaves. SERVES 4

JUMBO SHRIMP WITH GARLIC AND GINGER

Look for raw tiger prawns or use ordinary jumbo shrimp.

1 pound LARGE, RAW SHELLED JUMBO SHRIMP OR TIGER PRAWNS
2 tablespoons VEGETABLE OIL
4 cloves GARLIC, FINELY CHOPPED
1¹/₂-inch piece FRESH GINGERROOT, FINELY CHOPPED
grated peel of 1 LIME
2 teaspoons ASIAN FISH SAUCE OR SOY SAUCE
4 SCALLIONS, THINLY SLICED

Rinse and dry the shrimp on paper towels. Use a skillet large enough to hold the shrimp in a single layer. Heat the oil, add the garlic and ginger and gently cook for 1 minute.

Turn up the heat and add the shrimp. Turn them in the pan and fry them long enough to turn pink, about 2 minutes. Stir in the lime peel and fish sauce and 2 tablespoons water. Simmer for 1 minute. Stir in the scallions. Serve immediately. SERVES 4

TOP: *Haddock with Lime and Cilantro*
BOTTOM: *Jumbo Shrimp with Garlic and Ginger*

Meat and Poultry

Garlic can be added in abundance to many meat dishes to achieve rich, strong flavors which satisfy the healthiest of appetites. Try gremolata – finely chopped parsley, lemon peel and garlic – with turkey steaks or in casseroles, or add a little raw garlic to a cooked dish as a final flourish.

Chicken with 50 Cloves of Garlic

The garlic imparts a delicious aroma to the chicken – even more than 50 cloves can be used. The cooked cloves taste mild and nutty; they can be squeezed from their skins and eaten with accompanying vegetables.

1 x 3- to 3¹/₂-pound CHICKEN
¹/₂ LEMON
sprigs THYME OR ROSEMARY
50 *cloves* GARLIC, UNPEELED
4 *tablespoons* OLIVE OIL
SALT AND PEPPER
2 *tablespoons* ALL-PURPOSE FLOUR

Preheat the oven to 375°F. Stuff the chicken with the lemon and some thyme. Place in an earthenware casserole or baking dish with a lid. Remove the papery outer skins from the garlic. Add to the dish, then pour the oil over making sure the chicken and garlic are coated. Scatter some more herbs over and season.

Mix the flour with enough water to form a dough, then roll it out into a thin roll. Moisten the rim of the cooking pot with water, then press the dough onto the edge. Put on the lid and the dough will create a seal. Cook in the oven for 1¹/₂ hours. Serve the chicken with the cloves of garlic. SERVES 4

Greek Lamb and Pasta Bake

Orzo is pasta shaped like grains of rice, available from Italian food stores. The garlic melts into the pasta during cooking, giving the dish a rich, satisfying taste. The dish is ready when the pasta is tender.

8 SMALL LEAN LAMB SIRLOIN CHOPS
4 LARGE CLOVES GARLIC, HALVED OR QUARTERED
2¹/₂ *cups* STOCK
1 x 14-*ounce* CAN CRUSHED TOMATOES
3 *tablespoons* EXTRA-VIRGIN OLIVE OIL
2 *teaspoons* DRIED OREGANO
1¹/₃ *cups* ORZO

Preheat the oven to 400°F. Place the chops in a large baking dish in a single layer. Scatter the pieces of garlic over, pour half the stock over and add the tomatoes, oil and oregano. Season to taste, cover and place in the oven. Cook for 45 minutes.

Remove from the oven, pour the remaining stock over and stir in the orzo; ensure it is covered in liquid. Return to the oven for 40 minutes. Stir once or twice while cooking. SERVES 4

RIGHT: Chicken with 50 Cloves of Garlic

GARLIC ROAST PORK

If the crumb crust falls off during carving, spoon onto the slices of roast pork to serve.

1 x 3-pound BONED PORK TOP LOIN ROAST
6 large cloves GARLIC, FINELY CHOPPED
3 tablespoons CHOPPED FRESH PARSLEY
1 teaspoon CHOPPED ROSEMARY NEEDLES
SALT AND PEPPER
1/3 cup FINELY CHOPPED COOKED HAM
3 tablespoons OLIVE OIL
2/3 cup DRY WHITE WINE
2 cups CHICKEN STOCK
1 cup FRESH WHITE BREAD CRUMBS
1 tablespoon CORNSTARCH

Trim off the rind and as much fat as possible from the pork. Preheat the oven to 400°F. Mix the garlic, parsley and rosemary together. Season with salt and pepper. Mix half this mixture with the ham.

Open out the pork and spread the ham mixture over it. Roll up and tie with string. Brush the joint with 1 tablespoon of the oil. Place in a roasting pan, underside up. Roast for 30 minutes. Turn the joint over and add the wine and 2/3 cup of the stock. Baste the meat. Roast for 30 minutes longer.

Meanwhile, mix the remaining garlic mixture with the bread crumbs and remaining oil. Remove the joint from the oven, cut off the strings and press the crumb mixture all over the pork. Lower the oven temperature to 350°F and roast for 40 minutes until the crust is golden and crisp. Transfer the joint to a carving board.

Pour the remaining stock into the pan and scrape up any brown pieces of meat. Blend the cornstarch with 3 tablespoons water, add to pan and simmer the gravy to thicken. Strain into a gravy boat. Carve the pork and serve with the gravy. SERVES 4-6

SPICY COCONUT AND CHICKEN CURRY

1 ONION, ROUGHLY CHOPPED
5 large cloves GARLIC, ROUGHLY CHOPPED
2 stalks LEMONGRASS
1 or 2 SMALL RED CHILIES, SEEDED AND ROUGHLY CHOPPED
1 x 2-inch piece FRESH GINGERROOT, PEELED AND CHOPPED
2 tablespoons PAPRIKA
1/2 teaspoon GROUND CORIANDER
1 teaspoon GROUND CUMIN
1/4 teaspoon TURMERIC
2 tablespoons VEGETABLE OIL
8 CHICKEN THIGHS, SKINNED AND BONED
1 x 14-ounce CAN COCONUT MILK
small bunch FRESH CILANTRO, TO GARNISH

Put the onion, garlic, the bottom 4 inches of the lemongrass, the chilies and ginger in a blender or food processor. Add the ground spices and blend to a paste.

In a large skillet, heat the oil and cook the paste for 4-5 minutes. Cut the chicken thighs into chunks, add to the pan and stir in the mixture to coat. Add the coconut milk and simmer uncovered for 25-30 minutes until the chicken is tender and the juices run clear, stirring occasionally. Shred the cilantro leaves and garnish. Serve with rice.

SERVES 4

RIGHT: Garlic Roast Pork

STEAK PIZZAIOLA

3 tablespoons OLIVE OIL
1 SMALL ONION, THINLY SLICED
4 cloves GARLIC, SLICED
1 x 14-ounce CAN CRUSHED TOMATOES
1 teaspoon DRIED OREGANO OR BASIL
SALT AND PEPPER
4 x 7-ounce SIRLOIN STEAKS
2 tablespoons DRY WHITE WINE
8 RIPE OLIVES, PITTED AND SLICED
(OPTIONAL)

Heat 2 tablespoons of the oil in a sauté pan or skillet. Add the onion and cook for 3-4 minutes. Add the garlic and when it begins to turn golden, add the tomatoes and oregano or basil. Simmer for 12-15 minutes. Season with salt and pepper.

Heat a large heavy-bottomed skillet. Add the remaining oil, then the steaks and cook on both sides just enough to brown them. Pour the wine over, then the tomato sauce. Turn the steaks in the sauce, then cover the pan and simmer for 5 minutes. Serve the steaks, each topped with the sauce and olives, if using.

SERVES 4

TURKEY STEAKS MILANESE

Top the steaks with an aromatic mixture called gremolata just before serving so the aroma of the citrus peel is retained.

1 tablespoon BUTTER
2 tablespoons OLIVE OIL
4 TURKEY BREAST STEAKS
4 cloves GARLIC, HALVED
2/3 cup DRY WHITE WINE
1 1/4 cups WELL-FLAVORED TURKEY OR
CHICKEN STOCK
2 sprigs FRESH ROSEMARY OR
1 teaspoon DRIED ROSEMARY
1 teaspoon CORNSTARCH
5 tablespoons LIGHT CREAM
SALT AND PEPPER

Gremolata
2 tablespoons CHOPPED FRESH PARSLEY
grated peel of 1 LEMON
1 clove GARLIC, FINELY CHOPPED

Heat the butter and oil in a large skillet that will hold the turkey steaks in a single layer. Add the steaks and lightly brown on both sides. Add the garlic and when pale golden, pour off the excess fat. Add the wine and stock. Break the sprigs of rosemary into 2 or 3 pieces and add to the pan. Cover and simmer for 15-20 minutes until the turkey is tender and the juices run clear.

To make the gremolata, combine the parsley, lemon peel and chopped garlic; set aside. Transfer the turkey to a serving dish, keep warm. Remove the garlic and rosemary from the pan and discard. Blend the cornstarch with the cream and stir into the sauce. Simmer to thicken, then season to taste. Pour the sauce over the steaks and scatter the gremolata over.

SERVES 4

TOP: Steak Pizzaiola
BOTTOM: Turkey Steaks Milanese

MOROCCAN CHICKEN CASSEROLE

1 x 3¹/2-pound CHICKEN, CUT INTO 8 PIECES

4 tablespoons LEMON JUICE

3 tablespoons VIRGIN OLIVE OIL

1 tablespoon FINELY CHOPPED GARLIC

1 teaspoon GROUND GINGER

1 teaspoon GROUND CUMIN

1 teaspoon GROUND CORIANDER

1 teaspoon CINNAMON

large pinch SAFFRON THREADS

¹/2 teaspoon GROUND BLACK PEPPER

1 ONION, THINLY SLICED

2¹/2 cups CHICKEN STOCK

6 ounces READY-TO-EAT PRUNES, PITTED

2 teaspoons CORNSTARCH

small bunch CILANTRO LEAVES

Put the chicken pieces in a large baking dish, and pour the lemon juice and oil over, then scatter the garlic over. Marinate for 2-4 hours.

Preheat oven to 350°F. Mix the spices together, then sprinkle over the chicken. Add the onion and stock, then cover and cook in the oven for 1 hour.

Stir in the prunes and cook for 30 minutes longer. Blend the cornstarch with a little water and stir into the casserole. Add salt, if needed, and return to the oven for 15 minutes until the sauce has thickened. Shred the cilantro leaves and scatter over the casserole. Serve with steamed couscous.   SERVES 4

LAMB KOFTA WITH ONION AND GARLIC RELISH

1¹/2 pounds GROUND LAMB

1 ONION, GRATED

2 cloves GARLIC, FINELY CHOPPED

2 tablespoons CHOPPED FRESH PARSLEY

1 tablespoon CHOPPED FRESH CILANTRO

2 teaspoons GROUND CORIANDER

1 teaspoon GROUND CUMIN

¹/2 teaspoon CINNAMON

SALT AND PEPPER

Onion and Garlic Relish

4 tablespoons OLIVE OIL

3 cups THINLY SLICED ONIONS

1 tablespoon SUGAR

1 tablespoon FINELY CHOPPED GARLIC

2 tablespoons WHITE-WINE VINEGAR

Put all the ingredients for the kofta into a bowl. Season to taste. Knead the mixture by hand until it looks paste-like. Cover and refrigerate for 2 hours.

Meanwhile, make the relish. Heat the oil in a heavy-bottomed skillet. Add the onions and sugar and cook until softened and golden. Stir in the garlic and cook for 1 minute. Add the vinegar and continue to cook until almost all of the liquid has evaporated and the onions are tender. Season and then set aside. Preheat the broiler.

Divide the lamb mixture into 16 portions, and roll each portion into a link sausage shape. Place on the broiler rack and cook under a medium-hot broiler for about 15 minutes, turning the koftas until browned all over. Serve with the warm relish and a salad.   SERVES 4

TOP: *Moroccan Chicken Casserole*

BOTTOM: *Lamb Kofta with Onion and Garlic Relish*

ORIENTAL CHICKEN WITH NOODLES

1¹/2 pounds SKINLESS, BONELESS CHICKEN BREAST
HALVES

4 tablespoons LIME JUICE

3 tablespoons SOY SAUCE

4 cloves GARLIC, FINELY CHOPPED

2 RED CHILIES, SEEDED AND FINELY
CHOPPED

1 teaspoon SUGAR

4 ounces CHINESE EGG NOODLES

2 tablespoons VEGETABLE OIL

4 SCALLIONS, TRIMMED AND CHOPPED,
OR MADE INTO FLOWERS, TO GARNISH

Chop the chicken into very small pieces. Put in a bowl with the lime juice, soy sauce, garlic, chilies and sugar. Stir, cover and set aside for 1 hour.

Bring a large pan of water to the boil, add the noodles, cover, then turn off the heat.

Heat the oil in a large wok or skillet. Add the chicken mixture and cook, stirring constantly for 5-6 minutes. Drain the noodles, then stir into the chicken mixture and stir together for 1 minute. Garnish and serve immediately.   SERVES 4

BEEF AND PEPPER STIR-FRY

8 ounces BROCCOLI

1 tablespoon SESAME OIL

1 tablespoon SUNFLOWER OIL

1 pound SIRLOIN STEAK, CUT INTO THIN STRIPS

1 RED BELL PEPPER, SEEDED AND THINLY
SLICED

1 YELLOW BELL PEPPER, SEEDED AND THINLY
SLICED

5 SCALLIONS, SLICED DIAGONALLY

1 tablespoon CHOPPED FRESH GINGERROOT

3 cloves GARLIC, THINLY SLICED

2 tablespoons DRY SHERRY

1/4 teaspoon CHINESE FIVE-SPICE POWDER

2 tablespoons SOY SAUCE

1 teaspoon CORNSTARCH

SESAME SEEDS (OPTIONAL)

Divide the broccoli into small flowerets and thinly slice the stems. Heat both oils in a wok or large skillet. Add the beef and brown for 2-3 minutes. Remove with a slotted spoon.

Add the vegetables to the pan with the ginger and garlic and stir-fry for 3-4 minutes. Stir in the sherry, five-spice powder and soy sauce, then return the beef to the pan. Blend the cornstarch with 3 tablespoons water, add to the pan and simmer until the sauce thickens. Transfer to a dish, sprinkle with sesame seeds, if wished, and serve with rice or noodles.   SERVES 4

TOP: *Oriental Chicken with Noodles*

BOTTOM: *Beef and Pepper Stir-Fry*

PROVENÇAL CASSOULET

For a variation, omit half of the fresh sausages and add 8 ounces smoked pork sausage cut into thick slices. French haricot beans are traditionally used in cassoulet, but navy and great northern beans taste good, too.

12 ounces BACON SLICES

1 x 8-ounce piece SMOKED HAM

4 tablespoons OLIVE OIL

1 pound COARSE PORK LINK SAUSAGES

1 LARGE ONION, CHOPPED

1/2 teaspoon CHILI POWDER

12 cloves GARLIC

1 x 14-ounce CAN CRUSHED TOMATOES

1 tablespoon TOMATO PASTE

2/3 cup DRY WHITE WINE

2 cups STOCK

bunch FRESH HERBS

1 x 15-ounce CAN HARICOT OR NAVY BEANS, DRAINED

1 x 15 1/2-ounce CAN LIMA OR FAVA BEANS, DRAINED

1 SMALL CRUSTY WHITE FRENCH LOAF

Preheat the oven to 325°F. Cut the pork and bacon into bite-size pieces. Heat half the oil in a large flameproof casserole, then add the pork, bacon and sausages and cook until lightly browned. Remove from the pan, cut the sausages into thirds and set aside. Stir the onion into the casserole and cook until golden. Stir in the chili powder and garlic and cook for 1 minute. Stir in the tomatoes, tomato paste, wine, stock, herbs and beans. Return the meats to the casserole (and sliced smoked pork sausage, if using). Bring the liquid to a boil, then cover and bake for 1 1/4 hours.

Meanwhile, make rough bread crumbs from the French bread and toss them in the remaining oil. Increase the oven temperature to 375°F. Remove the herbs from the casserole and sprinkle the bread crumbs over. Return, uncovered, to the oven for 30 minutes or until golden. SERVES 6

PORK CHOPS WITH GARLIC PEARLS AND MUSTARD SAUCE

4 BONELESS PORK LOIN CHOPS

SALT AND PEPPER

1 tablespoon DIJON MUSTARD

24 cloves GARLIC, PEELED

2/3 cup DRY WHITE WINE

2 cups CHICKEN STOCK

2 teaspoons CORNSTARCH

4 tablespoons LIGHT CREAM

1 teaspoon WHOLEGRAIN MUSTARD

Preheat the oven to 350°F. Season the chops and spread the mustard over them, then place in a baking dish. Arrange the garlic cloves around the chops. Pour the wine and stock over, cover and cook for 1 1/4 hours until the pork is tender. Transfer the chops to a warmed serving dish, keep warm. Strain the cooking juices into a pan, reserving the garlic, and boil for 5 minutes. Blend the cornstarch with the cream, stir into the pan with the mustard and simmer to thicken. To serve, place a chop on each plate, pour the sauce over and garnish with the garlic. SERVES 4

TOP: Provençal Cassoulet

BOTTOM: Pork Chops with Garlic Pearls and Mustard Sauce

ROAST LAMB WITH GARLIC AND ROSEMARY

The flavor of oak-smoked garlic is slightly milder than fresh garlic.

1 x 3 1/2-pound	LEG OF LAMB
16 small sprigs	FRESH ROSEMARY
1 or 2 cloves	GARLIC, CUT INTO 16 SLIVERS, PLUS 1 WHOLE HEAD
1 tablespoon	OLIVE OIL
	SALT AND PEPPER
2/3 cup	RED WINE
1 tablespoon	ALL-PURPOSE FLOUR
2 1/2 cups	LAMB STOCK

Preheat the oven to 400°F. Use the point of a sharp knife to make 16 slits all over the lamb and insert the sprigs of rosemary and slivers of garlic. Place in a roasting pan and brush the olive oil over; season. Separate the head of garlic into cloves. Peel, then tuck the cloves under the lamb.

Roast the lamb for 30 minutes. Reduce the oven temperature to 350°F. Pour the red wine over and roast for 1 hour longer, basting 2 or 3 times during roasting.

Transfer the lamb to a serving dish, cover and keep warm. Skim off the fat from the pan juices, crush the garlic and mash into the juices. Add the flour and cook for 1 minute on the stovetop. Add the stock, bring to a boil and simmer for 5 minutes. Season, then strain into a gravy boat.   SERVES 6

SPANISH CHICKEN CASSEROLE

3 tablespoons	OLIVE OIL
1 x 3 1/2-pound	CHICKEN, CUT INTO 8 PIECES
1	ONION, CHOPPED
2	RED BELL PEPPERS, SEEDED AND CUT INTO 1/2-INCH STRIPS
5 cloves	GARLIC, ROUGHLY CRUSHED
1/2 cup	DICED COOKED HAM
1 x 14-ounce	CAN CRUSHED TOMATOES
3/4 cup	MEDIUM-DRY SHERRY
1	BAY LEAF
1 teaspoon	DRIED MEDITERRANEAN HERBS
1/3 cup	RIPE OR GREEN OLIVES, PITTED

Heat the oil in a large, shallow flameproof casserole. Add the chicken pieces and cook until golden brown, then remove from the pan and set aside. Add the onion and cook for 5 minutes until golden. Add the peppers and stir until slightly softened. Stir in the garlic and ham and sauté for 1 minute. Stir in the tomatoes and sherry, then add the bay leaf, herbs and olives and simmer. Return the chicken to the casserole, cover and simmer for 1 1/2 hours.

Season and discard the bay leaf. If wished, the sauce can be thickened with 2 teaspoons cornstarch blended with a little water. Serve with rice or potatoes.   SERVES 4

TOP: Roast Lamb with Garlic and Rosemary
BOTTOM: Spanish Chicken Casserole

SIMPLE SUPPERS

Ideal for a light meal, these dishes can be served with crisp, green salads and farmhouse-style bread. The pasta meals are quick and easy and all the recipes make good use of everyday ingredients, including varying amounts of garlic.

MEXICAN CHILI PIE

2 tablespoons OIL
1 ONION, CHOPPED
3 cloves GARLIC, CRUSHED
1 pound COARSE LEAN GROUND BEEF
1 teaspoon GROUND CUMIN
1/2 teaspoon CHILI POWDER
2/3 cup BEEF STOCK
1 x 14-ounce CAN CRUSHED TOMATOES
1 GREEN BELL PEPPER, SEEDED AND DICED
1 tablespoon TOMATO PASTE
1 teaspoon DRIED OREGANO
1 x 15 1/2-ounce CAN MIXED OR RED KIDNEY BEANS, DRAINED
SALT AND PEPPER

Topping
3 tablespoons OLIVE OIL
6 cloves GARLIC, THINLY SLICED
1 SMALL FRENCH LOAF, THINLY SLICED
1/2 cup FINELY GRATED SHARP CHEDDAR CHEESE

Heat the oil in a large pan. Cook the onion until it starts to soften, then add the garlic and cook for 2 minutes. Stir in the beef and cook until browned. Add the spices and cook for 1 minute, then stir in the stock, tomatoes, pepper, tomato paste and oregano and simmer for 25 minutes, stirring occasionally. Add the beans and season to taste

Heat the oven to 375°F. Transfer the chili to a large gratin dish. Heat the oil for the topping, add the sliced garlic and cook slowly to soften. Remove from the heat, brush the bread with the oil, and arrange the slices on top of the chili. Scatter the slices of garlic and the grated cheese over, and then bake uncovered for 20 minutes.

SERVES 6

RIGHT: Mexican Chili Pie

GARLIC AND ONION TART

1¹/2 cups ALL-PURPOSE FLOUR

3 tablespoons MARGARINE

3 tablespoons SHORTENING

2 tablespoons BUTTER

3 cups THINLY SLICED ONIONS

1 head GARLIC, ROASTED (SEE PAGE 20)

2 EGGS

²/3 cup LIGHT CREAM

4 tablespoons MILK

CHOPPED FRESH PARSLEY, TO SERVE

Sift the flour into a bowl with a pinch of salt, then add the fats and cut in. Add 2-3 tablespoons iced water and press the mixture together to form a dough. Lightly knead, then cover and chill for 30 minutes. Preheat the oven to 400°F. Roll out the dough and line a lightly greased 9-inch tart pan. Prick the base all over. Line the pastry case with a piece of foil and bake for 15 minutes. Remove the foil and bake for 5 minutes longer. Remove from the oven. Reduce the heat to 350°F.

Melt the butter in a large skillet. Fry the onions for 20 minutes until soft, then remove from the heat. Squeeze garlic from the skins and mash, then beat with the eggs, cream and milk, season. Pour a little into the tart shell. Add the onions and remaining egg mixture. Return the tart to oven on a baking sheet and bake for 30 minutes until the filling is set. Sprinkle with chopped parsley.

SERVES 4-6

BROCCOLI AND MUSHROOM RISOTTO

It is important to use Italian arborio rice to achieve the creamy consistency required for a successful risotto.

8 ounces BROCCOLI

3 tablespoons OLIVE OIL

1 SMALL ONION, FINELY CHOPPED

2 cloves GARLIC, FINELY CHOPPED

1¹/2 cups ARBORIO RICE

²/3 cup DRY WHITE WINE

3 cups HOT CHICKEN OR VEGETABLE STOCK

2¹/4 cups QUARTERED BROWN MUSHROOMS

¹/2 cup FRESHLY GRATED PARMESAN CHEESE

SNIPPED FRESH CHIVES, TO GARNISH

Cut the broccoli into small flowerets and the stems into ¹/2-inch pieces. Blanch for 2 minutes; drain. Heat the oil in large pan, add the onion and garlic and cook until golden. Add the rice and cook, stirring until the grains are well coated with oil. Bring the wine and stock to a boil in a separate pan, then add half to the rice and cook for about 10 minutes over steady heat, stirring until the liquid is absorbed. Add the mushrooms, remaining liquid and cook for 10-15 minutes longer, adding more water if needed, until the rice is tender and the stock absorbed. Stir in the broccoli and heat for 1-2 minutes. Season. Remove from the heat and stir in the Parmesan. Garnish with chives and serve. SERVES 4

TOP: Broccoli and Mushroom Risotto
BOTTOM: Garlic and Onion Tart

SPAGHETTI WITH WALNUT AND PARSLEY SAUCE

3 large cloves GARLIC
1½ ounces PARSLEY SPRIGS
5 tablespoons VIRGIN OLIVE OIL
½ cup FRESHLY GRATED PARMESAN CHEESE
½ cup FINELY CHOPPED WALNUTS
5 tablespoons LIGHT CREAM
1 pound SPAGHETTI OR SPAGHETTINI

To Garnish
sprigs PARSLEY
FRESHLY GRATED PARMESAN CHEESE

Put the garlic and parsley in a blender or food processor and blend until finely chopped. Add the oil and blend to make a paste. Turn into a bowl and beat in the Parmesan cheese, walnuts and cream.

Cook the spaghetti in plenty of boiling salted water until *al dente*; drain well. Return to the pan, add the sauce and toss, then turn into a warmed serving bowl. Garnish with small sprigs of parsley and the extra Parmesan cheese. Serve immediately.   SERVES 4

CRÊPES WITH GARLIC-CHEESE FILLING

1 cup ALL-PURPOSE FLOUR
large pinch SALT
2 EGGS
1¼ cups MILK
2 tablespoons CHOPPED FRESH PARSLEY OR SNIPPED CHIVES
BUTTER FOR FRYING

Filling
3 tablespoons BUTTER
2 SHALLOTS, FINELY CHOPPED
5 cloves GARLIC, FINELY CHOPPED
1 cup RICOTTA CHEESE
½ cup CHOPPED MOZZARELLA CHEESE
¼ cup FRESHLY GRATED PARMESAN CHEESE

To make 8-10 crêpes, put the flour, salt, eggs and milk into a blender or food processor and blend until smooth. Add the parsley and mix in. To cook the crêpes, melt a small knob of butter in an 8-inch skillet. Pour in enough batter to coat the bottom of the pan. Cook the crêpe over medium-high heat until set and golden. Flip over and cook the other side until golden. Transfer to a plate or a tray and continue making crêpes until all batter is used.

Preheat the oven to 350°F. Melt 2 tablespoons of the butter in a small pan. Add the shallots and cook gently for 3 minutes, then add the garlic and cook for 1 minute. Stir into the ricotta cheese with the mozzarella. Place 1 tablespoon of the filling at one end of a crêpe, then fold over the sides and roll up. Place in a baking dish. Repeat with all the crêpes and filling. Melt the remaining butter and brush the crêpes with it. Scatter the Parmesan over and bake for 12-15 minutes until golden and hot.

SERVES 4

TOP: Spaghetti with Walnut and Parsley Sauce
BOTTOM: Crêpes with Garlic-Cheese Filling

GARLIC AND HERB SOUFFLÉ

If you can find garlic shoots, the young green stems of the plant, use these instead of chives.

4 ounces GARLIC CLOVES, PEELED
3 tablespoons BUTTER
1 tablespoon GRATED PARMESAN CHEESE
$^1/_2$ cup ALL-PURPOSE FLOUR
1 $^1/_4$ cups MILK, WARM
4 EGGS, SEPARATED
1 teaspoon DIJON MUSTARD
2 tablespoons CHOPPED FRESH PARSLEY
1 tablespoon SNIPPED CHIVES
$^3/_4$ cup GRATED SHARP CHEDDAR CHEESE
SALT AND PEPPER

To make the garlic purée, put the garlic in a small pan and cover with water, then simmer for about 20 minutes until tender; cool. Press through a strainer. Using 1 tablespoon of the butter, grease a 6 $^1/_4$-cup soufflé dish, then coat all over with the Parmesan cheese. Preheat the oven to 400°F.

Melt the remaining butter in a large saucepan. Blend in the flour and stir over low heat for 1 minute. Remove from the heat and gradually blend in the milk. Bring to a boil, stirring until thickened. Remove from the heat, beat in the egg yolks, one by one, then add the garlic purée, mustard, herbs and cheese; season lightly. Beat the egg whites until stiff, add one-third to the sauce and when fully mixed in, fold in the rest. Turn into the prepared dish. Reduce the oven temperature to 375°F. Cook for 25 minutes. Serve immediately. SERVES 3-4

GARLIC PIZZA

Using a ready-made pizza base mix saves time and gives a good result.

16 cloves GARLIC
1 x 7-ounce CAN CRUSHED TOMATOES
pinch SUGAR
SALT AND PEPPER
1 x 5-ounce PACKAGE PIZZA BASE MIXTURE
$^1/_4$ cup SLICED CHEDDAR CHEESE
$^1/_4$ cup SLICED GRUYÈRE OR MOZZARELLA CHEESE
$^1/_2$ teaspoon ITALIAN SEASONING
1 tablespoon OLIVE OIL

Place the garlic in a pan. Cover with water and simmer for 10 minutes; drain. Put the tomatoes in a pan with the sugar; season. Simmer until thick and pulpy. Preheat the oven to 425°F. Empty the pizza base mixture into a bowl. Chop 6 of the garlic cloves and add to the bowl with the water specified on package. Knead well on a floured surface for 5 minutes. Roll out into an 8-inch circle and place on a greased baking sheet. Spread the tomato mixture over. Arrange the cheese on top, then scatter the rest of the garlic over, halving any large cloves. Sprinkle with herbs and oil and bake for 10 minutes. If the top browns too fast, lower the heat to 375°F. Bake for 10 minutes longer until golden brown. SERVES 2

RIGHT: Garlic Pizza

TRICOLORE FRITTATA

This savory Mediterranean frittata captures the flavor and colors of a warm climate. Add a little chopped cooked ham, if wished.

3 *tablespoons* OLIVE OIL
1 ONION, SLICED
5 *cloves* GARLIC, SLICED
1 RED BELL PEPPER, SEEDED AND SLICED
1 GREEN BELL PEPPER, SEEDED AND SLICED
8 RIPE OLIVES, PITTED
8 EGGS
1 *tablespoon* CHOPPED FRESH PARSLEY
2 *tablespoons* FRESHLY GRATED PARMESAN CHEESE

Heat the oil in a large nonstick skillet. Add the onion and cook over medium-high heat for 5-6 minutes until it starts to turn golden. Stir in the garlic, peppers and olives and cook for 4 minutes longer, until the peppers begin to soften.

Beat the eggs with salt and pepper. Pour into the pan with the parsley, lower the heat and cook for 10-15 minutes until almost set; the top will still be a little runny. Meanwhile, preheat the broiler.

Scatter the Parmesan over, then place under a medium-hot broiler until the top is golden. Serve cut into wedges with a green salad.   SERVES 4

TAGLIATELLE WITH GARLIC, GORGONZOLA AND BASIL

SALT AND PEPPER
12 *ounces* TAGLIATELLE
4 *tablespoons* BUTTER
3 *cloves* GARLIC, SLICED
8 *ounces* GORGONZOLA CHEESE, CRUMBLED
2/3 *cup* LIGHT CREAM
2 *tablespoons* CHOPPED FRESH BASIL

Bring a large saucepan of salted water to a boil. Add the pasta and boil for 10-12 minutes until *al dente*.

Meanwhile, melt the butter in a pan. Add the garlic and cook for 2 minutes. Add half of the gorgonzola cheese to the pan with the cream and stir over low heat until the cheese has melted. Add the basil and season with pepper, if needed.

Drain the pasta, divide between warmed serving plates, pour the sauce over and scatter the remaining gorgonzola over. Serve immediately.   SERVES 4

TOP: Tricolore Frittata
BOTTOM: Tagliatelle with Garlic, Gorgonzola and Basil

CARROT AND LENTIL PATTIES

Serve these patties with a refreshing yogurt sauce flavored with garlic according to taste.

1¹/2 *cups* RED LENTILS

1 *tablespoon* OLIVE OIL

1 SMALL ONION, FINELY CHOPPED

1 ¹/3 *cups* VERY FINELY CHOPPED CARROTS

2 *cloves* GARLIC, FINELY CHOPPED

2 *teaspoons* GROUND CUMIN

¹/2 *teaspoon* CAYENNE PEPPER

4 *tablespoons* CHOPPED FRESH PARSLEY

1 *cup* FRESH BREAD CRUMBS

1 EGG, BEATEN

Sauce

³/4 *cup* PLAIN YOGURT

1 *or* 2 *cloves* GARLIC, CRUSHED

1 *teaspoon* LEMON JUICE

Put the lentils in a large pan of salted water and bring to a boil, then simmer for 15 minutes until tender; drain. Put into a bowl and mash lightly.

Heat the oil, add the onion and cook until golden, add the carrots and garlic and cook for 3 minutes longer. Stir in the cumin and cayenne. Add to the lentils and mix in 3 tablespoons of the parsley, the bread crumbs and egg; season. Shape the mixture into 12 patties, place on a tray and chill.

Combine all the ingredients for the sauce, plus the remaining parsley. Cover and refrigerate until needed.

To cook the patties, brush them on both sides with oil, place on a foil-lined broiler pan and broil for 3-4 minutes on both sides until golden brown, turning them carefully. Serve with the yogurt-garlic sauce.   MAKES 12

EGGPLANT AND TOMATO BAKE

Look in Italian food stores and delicatessens for cartons of imported puréed and strained tomatoes.

1 *tablespoon* OLIVE OIL, PLUS EXTRA FOR BRUSHING

1 ONION, FINELY CHOPPED

3 *large cloves* GARLIC, FINELY CHOPPED

2 *cups* PURÉED AND STRAINED TOMATOES

1¹/2 *teaspoons* CHOPPED FRESH THYME OR

¹/2 *teaspoon* DRIED THYME

SALT AND PEPPER

1¹/2 *pounds* EGGPLANT, CUT INTO ¹/4-INCH SLICES

2 BEEFSTEAK TOMATOES, SKINNED AND THINLY SLICED

³/4 *cup* FRESHLY GRATED PARMESAN CHEESE

Preheat the oven to 350°F. Heat 1 tablespoon oil in a skillet. Add the onion and gently cook until soft. Add the garlic and cook for 1 minute. Stir in the strained tomatoes and thyme and simmer for 10 minutes; season to taste.

Lightly brush each eggplant slice with oil, place under a hot broiler and broil on both sides until just beginning to turn golden. Arrange a layer of these slices, overlapping slightly, in an oiled gratin dish. Spoon one-third of the sauce over, add a layer of sliced tomato, then scatter 2 tablespoons of the cheese over. Repeat the layers finishing with eggplant. Brush with oil, then scatter the rest of the cheese over. Cover with foil and bake for 1¹/4 hours.   SERVES 6

TOP: *Carrot and Lentil Patties*

BOTTOM: *Eggplant and Tomato Bake*

VEGETABLES

The emphasis of this chapter is on fresh vegetables, which are cooked in various ways to enhance their flavor. All the dishes complement grilled, broiled or roasted meats; some, such as Char-Roasted Summer Vegetables, can also be served as a vegetarian main course.

GARLIC ROSTI

1¹/₂ pounds WAXY POTATOES
SALT
4 tablespoons BUTTER
1 MEDIUM ONION, FINELY CHOPPED
5 cloves GARLIC, FINELY CHOPPED

Peel the potatoes and cut into equal-size pieces. Boil in salted water for 10 minutes; drain and cool.

Preheat the oven to 375°F. Melt the butter in a large pan. Add the onion and cook for 4-5 minutes until it starts to soften. Add the garlic and cook for 1 minute. Coarsely grate the potatoes (a blender or food processor is very useful here), then stir into the pan and mix with the onion and garlic; season to taste. Divide the mixture into 12 and place in muffin pans. Bake for 35-40 minutes until crisp and golden. Serve as an accompaniment to roasted meats or poultry.   SERVES 4

BAKED TOMATOES WITH GARLIC CRUMBS

8-12 RIPE FIRM TOMATOES
SALT
4 tablespoons OLIVE OIL
4 cloves GARLIC, CRUSHED
1¹/₂ cups FINE FRESH WHITE BREAD CRUMBS
2 tablespoons CHOPPED FRESH PARSLEY

Preheat the oven to 350°F. Halve the tomatoes and season with salt. Stand them, cut sides up, in a baking dish. Heat the oil in a large sauté pan, add the garlic and bread crumbs and stir over medium heat for 3-4 minutes until light golden brown. Stir in the parsley, then divide between the tomatoes, pressing down slightly. Bake for 25-30 minutes until the tomatoes are soft but still hold their shape and the tops are crisp.   SERVES 4-6

TOP: Garlic Rosti
BOTTOM: Baked Tomatoes with Garlic Crumbs

BRAISED ROOT VEGETABLES WITH GARLIC

2 *tablespoons* OLIVE OIL

2 *tablespoons* BUTTER

1 ONION, QUARTERED

1½ *cups* CARROTS CUT INTO BATONS 1½ INCHES LONG

1½ *cups* PARSNIPS CUT INTO BATONS 1½ INCHES LONG

1½ *cups* PEELED AND CUBED CELERY ROOT

2 *cups* PEELED AND CUBED RUTABAGA

6 *ounces* SMALL NEW POTATOES, SCRUBBED

4-6 *heads* GARLIC

SALT AND PEPPER

2/3 *cup* VEGETABLE STOCK

Preheat the oven to 350°F. Heat the oil and the butter in a large, shallow flameproof casserole. Add the vegetables and cook over high heat until lightly browned. Remove from the heat. Rub off the outside papery skins of the garlic, and slice about 1 inch off the tops, then embed them in the vegetables. Season to taste. Add the stock, cover and cook for 45 minutes to 1 hour until the vegetables are tender.

Serve each portion with a head of garlic to be squeezed onto the vegetables while eating.   SERVES 4-6

GARLIC MASHED POTATOES

2 *heads* GARLIC (ABOUT 20 CLOVES)

1½ *pounds* POTATOES, PEELED

4 *tablespoons* BUTTER

SALT AND PEPPER

Peel the cloves of garlic and put in a large saucepan with the potatoes. Cover with water and boil until soft. Drain; retain the flavored water for a soup base, if wished.

Mash the potatoes with the butter, season with salt and pepper and beat until creamy.   SERVES 4-6

RIGHT: Braised Root Vegetables with Garlic

GREEN BEANS WITH GARLIC

8 ounces FRENCH-STYLE GREEN BEANS, TOPPED AND
TAILED

2 tablespoons BUTTER

3 cloves GARLIC, FINELY CHOPPED

grated peel and juice of 1/2 LEMON

SALT AND PEPPER

Halve the beans across the middle. Steam for 5-6 minutes until just tender.

Meanwhile, melt the butter in a small pan. Add the garlic and cook gently until light golden. Swirl in the lemon peel and juice. Season lightly. Put the beans in a serving dish, pour the mixture over and toss. Any left-overs can be added to a salad the next day.   SERVES 4

ZUCCHINI AND PEPPER GRATIN

2 pounds ZUCCHINI, CUT INTO 1/4-INCH SLICES

2 tablespoons BUTTER

1 ONION, SLICED

1 LARGE RED BELL PEPPER, SEEDED AND
SLICED

4 cloves GARLIC, FINELY CHOPPED

3 cups SKINNED, SEEDED AND CHOPPED
RIPE TOMATOES,

2 tablespoons CHOPPED FRESH BASIL

SALT AND PEPPER

1 tablespoon OLIVE OIL

3/4 cup GRATED GRUYÈRE CHEESE

1/2 cup FRESH BREAD CRUMBS

Put the zucchini in a large colander, sprinkle with salt and leave to drain for 30 minutes. Rinse and pat dry on paper towels.

Preheat the oven to 375°F. Melt the butter in a large pan. Add the onion and cook until soft and golden. Add the pepper and cook for 3 minutes longer. Stir in the garlic and tomatoes and simmer for about 10 minutes. Stir in the basil and season to taste.

Spread one-third of the zucchini on the bottom of a large, greased gratin dish, then spoon half the tomato mixture over. Repeat the layers and finish with a layer of zucchini. Brush the top with oil, cover and bake for 45 minutes.

Remove the foil, scatter the cheese and the bread crumbs over and return to the oven for 15 minutes. Serve with grilled, broiled or roast chicken or meat.

SERVES 6

TOP: Green Beans with Garlic

BOTTOM: Zucchini and Pepper Gratin

CHAR-ROASTED SUMMER VEGETABLES

A colorful mixture of Mediterranean vegetables baked in the oven until tender. Serve with broiled or barbecued meat and chicken.

2 ZUCCHINI, THICKLY SLICED DIAGONALLY

1 EGGPLANT, CUT INTO LARGE CHUNKS

4 SMALL RED ONIONS, HALVED

1 RED BELL PEPPER, SEEDED AND CUT INTO LARGE CHUNKS

1 YELLOW BELL PEPPER, SEEDED AND CUT INTO LARGE CHUNKS

1 x 14-ounce CAN ARTICHOKE HALVES, DRAINED AND HALVED

3 tablespoons OLIVE OIL

20 cloves GARLIC, PEELED

Put the zucchini and eggplant into a large colander, sprinkle with salt and set aside for 1 hour. Rinse and squeeze them and dry on paper towels.

Preheat the oven to 450°F. Put all the vegetables in a large, shallow baking dish. Drizzle the olive oil over and scatter the garlic over. Toss and spread out the vegetables in a single layer. Bake for 25 minutes until lightly charred. SERVES 4

GARLIC ROASTED POTATOES

2 pounds SMALL NEW POTATOES, SCRUBBED

3 tablespoons OLIVE OIL

2 tablespoons CHOPPED GARLIC (ABOUT 10 CLOVES)

COARSELY MILLED SEA SALT

Preheat the oven to 400°F. Put the potatoes in a pan of cold water, cutting them in half or quarters if they are more than 3 inches in diameter. Bring to a boil and simmer for 5 minutes; drain well.

Heat the oil in a roasting pan in the oven. Add the potatoes and turn in the oil until coated all over, then scatter the garlic over. Roast for approximately 30-35 minutes or until the potatoes are golden and crisp. Season with salt before serving. SERVES 4-6

RIGHT: Char-Roasted Summer Vegetables

OUTDOOR EATING

When the weather is fine, there is no nicer way to eat than *al fresco,* and the picnic ideas can be enjoyed without going further than a balcony or the local park. Garlic plays an essential part in the barbecue marinades, infusing meat or vegetables with a mouthwatering flavor.

PARMESAN-GARLIC TWISTS

Serve these golden-baked garlic twists at picnics and barbecues.

3 *tablespoons* BUTTER

3 *cloves* GARLIC, CRUSHED

9 *ounces* PUFF PASTRY DOUGH, THAWED IF FROZEN

4 *tablespoons* FRESHLY GRATED PARMESAN CHEESE

Preheat the oven to 400°F. Melt the butter, add the garlic and cook gently. Roll out the dough on a lightly floured surface to a 10- x 4-inch rectangle. Brush two-thirds of the garlic butter over, then sprinkle with half the cheese. Fold the pastry over from a wide side and roll again to make a piece 8 x 12 inches. Brush the remaining garlic butter over and scatter the remaining cheese over, pressing down lightly. Cut strips about 3/4 inch wide and 8 inches long. Twist and place on greased baking trays. Bake for about 12 minutes.   MAKES ABOUT 30

CORNMEAL, CHEESE AND GARLIC MUFFINS

5 *cloves* GARLIC, PEELED

2 *tablespoons* OLIVE OIL

1 *cup* SELF-RISING FLOUR

1 *tablespoon* BAKING POWDER

1/4 *teaspoon* CAYENNE PEPPER

1 *teaspoon* SALT

2 *cups* FINE CORNMEAL OR POLENTA

1 *cup* GRATED SHARP CHEDDAR CHEESE

4 *tablespoons* BUTTER, MELTED

2 LARGE EGGS, BEATEN

1¼ *cups* MILK

Make a garlic purée following the method on page 72 for Herb and Garlic Soufflé; set aside. Preheat the oven to 400°F.

Sift the flour, baking powder, cayenne and salt into a bowl, then stir in the cornmeal and cheese. Beat the melted butter, eggs, milk and garlic purée together. Pour onto the dry ingredients and mix quickly until just combined.

Spoon the batter into 12 well-greased muffin molds. Bake for 20 minutes until risen and golden brown. Cool a few minutes before turning the muffins onto a wire rack to completely cool.   MAKES 12

TOP: Parmesan-Garlic Twists

BOTTOM: Cornmeal, Cheese and Garlic Muffins

TOMATO AND GARLIC TART

Crust
2 cups ALL-PURPOSE FLOUR

pinch SALT

1 EGG, BEATEN

4 tablespoons OLIVE OIL

Filling
4 tablespoons OLIVE OIL

3 cups THINLY SLICED ONIONS

1 x 14-ounce CAN CRUSHED TOMATOES

1/2 teaspoon DRIED BASIL

1/2 teaspoon DRIED THYME

pinch DRIED ROSEMARY

6 cloves GARLIC, SLICED

1 1/2 pounds TOMATOES, SLICED

1 tablespoon CHOPPED FRESH PARSLEY, TO GARNISH

Put the flour and salt into a bowl and make a well in the center. Add the egg, oil and 3 tablespoons warm water. Mix well until the mixture forms a dough. Knead on a lightly floured surface, form into a ball, cover with plastic wrap and set aside for 30 minutes. Meanwhile, preheat the oven to 400°F. Grease an 11-inch tart pan.

Roll out the dough. Heat half the oil in a large skillet. Add the onions and cook for about 8 minutes until golden. Add the tomatoes and herbs and cook quickly until the liquid has evaporated. Spoon into the tart shell. Scatter the garlic over. Arrange the tomatoes on top and brush with the remaining oil. Season. Bake for 30 minutes, then reduce the oven temperature to 350°F and bake for 15 minutes longer.

Scatter the parsley over and serve.   SERVES 8

GARLICKY CHICKEN LIVER PÂTÉ

Smoked chicken or turkey breast is available at delicatessen counters in supermarkets. It adds a slightly smokey flavor to the pâté and gives it a light texture.

1 pound CHICKEN LIVERS

4 tablespoons BUTTER OR MARGARINE

2 SHALLOTS OR

1 SMALL ONION, SKINNED AND CHOPPED

4 cloves GARLIC, CRUSHED

6 ounces SMOKED CHICKEN OR TURKEY BREAST

2 tablespoons MEDIUM-DRY SHERRY

6 tablespoons WHIPPING CREAM, WHIPPED

SALT AND PEPPER

Wash the chicken livers and remove any green pieces, then cut in half and dry on paper towels. Melt the butter in a skillet. Add the onion and garlic and cook for about 5 minutes until the onion is softened. Add the chicken livers and cook for about 5 minutes until lightly golden on the outside but still pink inside. Leave to cool, then transfer to the bowl of a blender or food processor. Add the chicken or turkey breast, the sherry and the cream. Purée, then season. Spoon into a dish, level the top, cover and refrigerate.

Serve with Melba toast or French bread.   SERVES 8

RIGHT: Tomato and Garlic Tart

CROSTINI WITH ROASTED GARLIC PURÉE

Serve crostini as an appetizer at a barbecue. The bread can be toasted on the grid to give it a smokey flavor.

1 LOAF BREAD SUCH AS CIABATTA FRENCH BREAD

2 *large heads* GARLIC, ROASTED (SEE PAGE 20)

2 *tablespoons* OLIVE OIL

SALT AND PEPPER

5 *ounces* SOFT GOAT CHEESE

SMALL BASIL LEAVES, TO GARNISH

Cut the bread into $1/2$-inch slices and toast lightly on both sides. Squeeze the garlic cloves to remove the soft centers and mix the garlic purée with the oil. Season.

Spread over the toast and top with goat cheese, then place under the broiler to heat through. Garnish with basil leaves and serve. SERVES 4-6 AS AN APPETIZER OR SNACK

VEGETABLE KEBABS WITH RED PEPPER SALSA

1 LARGE ZUCCHINI, TOPPED AND TAILED

16 SMALL FIRM TOMATOES

8 BROWN MUSHROOMS

1 GREEN BELL PEPPER, SEEDED AND CUT INTO CHUNKS

1 YELLOW OR ORANGE PEPPER, SEEDED AND CUT INTO CHUNKS

8 PEARL ONIONS, OR 2 SMALL ONIONS, QUARTERED

Basting mixture

3 *tablespoons* OLIVE OIL

3 *cloves* GARLIC, CRUSHED

1 *tablespoon* LEMON JUICE

$1/2$ *teaspoon* DRIED THYME

Salsa

2 RED BELL PEPPERS, SEEDED AND ROUGHLY CHOPPED

3 *tablespoons* OLIVE OIL

3 *cloves* GARLIC

1 *tablespoon* RED-WINE VINEGAR

8 SUN-DRIED TOMATOES IN OIL, DRAINED

1 SMALL RED ONION, ROUGHLY CHOPPED

2 *tablespoons* CHOPPED FRESH PARSLEY

Halve the zucchini lengthwise and cut into $1/2$-inch slices. Thread onto skewers with the tomatoes, mushrooms, chunks of pepper and onions. Combine the ingredients for the basting mixture and brush the vegetables.

For the salsa, put the peppers in a blender or food processor with the oil, garlic, vinegar, sun-dried tomatoes and onion. Blend until very finely chopped. Season and add parsley.

Cook the kebabs on a prepared barbecue, turning them and brushing with the baste. Serve with the salsa.

SERVES 4

TOP: *Crostini with Roasted Garlic Purée*
BOTTOM: *Vegetable Kebabs with Red Pepper Salsa*

BARBECUED RED MULLETS WITH SKORDALIÀ

Skordalià is a pungent Greek sauce to serve with fish and vegetables. A wire basket is useful for cooking a whole fish on a barbecue.

4 x 7-ounce RED MULLETS, DRAWN
SALT AND PEPPER
4 tablespoons BUTTER
1 clove GARLIC, CRUSHED
1 tablespoon CHOPPED FRESH HERBS

Skordalià
1¹/₂ cups FRESH WHITE BREAD CRUMBS
4 cloves GARLIC
¹/₂ cup OLIVE OIL
1 tablespoon WHITE-WINE VINEGAR
¹/₂ cup BLANCHED ALMONDS, FINELY GROUND

To make the skordalià, put the bread crumbs in a bowl and moisten with water. Crush the garlic with a little salt until pulpy. Squeeze the water from the bread and put the bread in a blender or food processor with the garlic. With the motor running, slowly add the oil, then the vinegar. Turn into a bowl and stir in the ground almonds. (For a thinner sauce add a little lemon juice or light cream.)

Wash and scale the fish. Cut 2 slashes on each side and season with salt and pepper. Melt the butter and stir in the garlic and herbs. Brush this mixture over the fish. Cook the fish on a prepared barbecue for about 10 minutes, turning to cook them through. Serve with a bowl of the skordalià. SERVES 4

MEDITERRANEAN LAMB CHOPS

Choose boneless chops or leg steaks if preferred. Serve with green salad.

8 SMALL BONELESS LAMB SIRLOIN OR LOIN CHOPS

Marinade
6 cloves GARLIC, CRUSHED
2 tablespoons TOMATO PASTE
4 tablespoons OLIVE OIL
2 tablespoons RED-WINE VINEGAR
2 teaspoons PAPRIKA
2 tablespoons CHOPPED FRESH ROSEMARY OR MINT
2 teaspoons CORIANDER SEEDS, CRUSHED
FRESH HERBS, TO GARNISH

Put the chops in a glass dish. Mix the ingredients for the marinade together, then spread half of it over the chops. Turn the chops over and coat with the rest of the mixture. Cover and refrigerate for at least 2 hours or overnight.

Bring to room temperature before cooking. Place the chops on a prepared barbecue and cook for about 15 minutes, turning them half way through. SERVES 4

TOP: *Barbecued Red Mullets with Skordalià*
BOTTOM: *Mediterranean Lamb Chops*

SPICY SPARERIBS

These barbecued ribs are not too spicy so they will be popular with children.

3 pounds PORK SPARERIBS

Marinade
6-8 cloves GARLIC, CRUSHED
6 tablespoons CATSUP
6 tablespoons CIDER VINEGAR
4 tablespoons SUNFLOWER OIL
1 tablespoon WORCESTERSHIRE SAUCE
2 tablespoons BROWN SUGAR
2-3 tablespoons BOTTLED CHILI SAUCE
1 teaspoon GROUND CUMIN
1 teaspoon DIJON MUSTARD
1/2 teaspoon GROUND ALLSPICE

Put the ribs in a large shallow dish. Put all the marinade ingredients in a blender or food processor with 6 tablespoons water and blend until smooth. Pour over the ribs and ensure they are all coated with the marinade. Cover and refrigerate for at least 2 hours, preferably overnight. Bring to room temperature before cooking.

Lift the ribs from the marinade, place on a prepared barbecue and cook for 25-35 minutes over medium-hot coals. Turn the ribs often to prevent them from burning and brush with the marinade.   SERVES 4-6

THAI GARLIC CHICKEN

4 BONELESS CHICKEN BREAST HALVES

Marinade
4 cloves GARLIC, SLICED
1 tablespoon FINELY CHOPPED FRESH GINGERROOT
juice and grated peel of 1 LIME
3 tablespoons SUNFLOWER OIL
1 tablespoon SOY SAUCE
1 or 2 RED CHILIES, SEEDED AND THINLY SLICED
2 tablespoons CHOPPED FRESH CILANTRO

Cut 2 or 3 slashes in the chicken skin, then put the pieces in a glass dish. Mix the ingredients for the marinade and pour over the chicken, then cover and refrigerate for at least 2 hours. Bring to room temperature before cooking.

Lift the chicken from the marinade and place on a prepared barbecue and cook over medium-hot heat for 15-20 minutes, depending on the size of the chicken breast halves. Turn them over and brush with a little marinade to keep them moist while grilling.   SERVES 4

RIGHT: Thai Garlic Chicken

INDEX